BLIND
MAN'S
BLUFF

ALSO BY JAMES TATE HILL

Academy Gothic

BLIND MAN'S BLUFF

A Memoir

JAMES TATE HILL

W. W. NORTON & COMPANY
Independent Publishers Since 1923

"All the Answers" was originally published in slightly different form in *Waxwing*, Fall 2018, issue 16.

"Real Books" was originally published in slightly different form as "Do Audiobooks Count as Reading?" in *Literary Hub*, January 11, 2018.

"Pass/Fail" was originally published in slightly different form in *Prairie Schooner*, Summer 2019, vol. 93. no. 2, pp. 45–55.

Sections of "The D-Word" were originally published in different form in "My First VHS: *Rain Man*," *Hobart*, July 6, 2019.

Portions from the book were published in different form as "How Prince Helped Me Feel Seen" in *Literary Hub*, June 7, 2018.

For information about permission to reproduce selections from this book, write to Permissions, W. W. Norton & Company, Inc., 500 Fifth Avenue, New York, NY 10110

For information about special discounts for bulk purchases, please contact W. W. Norton Special Sales at specialsales@wwnorton.com or 800-233-4830

Manufacturing by Lake Book Manufacturing
Book design by Beth Steidle
Production manager: Beth Steidle

Library of Congress Cataloging-in-Publication Data

Names: Hill, James Tate, author.
Title: Blind man's bluff : a memoir / James Tate Hill.
Description: First edition. | New York, NY : W.W. Norton & Company, [2021]
Identifiers: LCCN 2021007014 | ISBN 9780393867176 (hardcover) |
    ISBN 9780393867183 (epub)
Subjects: LCSH: Hill, James Tate. | Blind—United States—Biography. | Blind
    authors—United States—Biography. | Deception.
Classification: LCC HV1792.H54 A3 2021 | DDC 813/.6 [B]—dc23
LC record available at https://lccn.loc.gov/2021007014

W. W. Norton & Company, Inc., 500 Fifth Avenue, New York, N.Y. 10110
www.wwnorton.com

W. W. Norton & Company Ltd., 15 Carlisle Street, London W1D 3BS

1 2 3 4 5 6 7 8 9 0

For my parents
and for Lori

Writers, unlike most people,
tell their best lies when they are alone.
—Michael Chabon, *Wonder Boys*

CONTENTS

AUTHOR'S NOTE

The events depicted in these pages are based on my own recollections. Conversations have been reconstructed to the best of my abilities, and certain names and identifying characteristics have been changed. In a few cases, incidents have been compressed to accommodate the narrative flow.

BLIND
MAN'S
BLUFF

PROLOGUE

IT'S FULL DARK WHEN we reach Nashville in December. Mom reads me the names of stores and restaurants as she drives, trying her best to feign excitement.

"Looks like you've got an Olive Garden," she says.

The jewel of my new neighborhood is a mall with a JCPenney, a Baptist church, and a bookstore that only sells remaindered books. Even if I want to leave my apartment, the lack of sidewalks means navigating around a four-lane highway. Never leaving the apartment sounds like a better idea.

I call my wife, Meredith, to say we're close. She's making mulled wine with a bottle of our wedding Cabernet.

"Shouldn't we save that for a special occasion?" I ask.

"You moving here isn't a special occasion?"

Shortly after accepting my marriage proposal, Meredith took an editing job that paid twice what I earned as an adjunct instructor of composition. We married in September and lived apart while I taught one final semester in North Carolina.

"I don't really like mulled wine," I say.

"Does your mom?"

"I don't think so," I say, not bothering to check with her.

My wife is all smiles when she answers the door. She hugs her mother-in-law while I carry boxes to the corner of the living room. I used to envy Meredith's outgoing personality. In light of recent events, I no longer trust her good moods.

"I can't believe we got married," my wife told me one night in early November, two months after we were married.

"What?"

She repeated what she had said.

"What are you talking about? Where is this coming from?"

She had trouble explaining.

I hung up on her. Moments later, unsatisfied by the fecklessness of hanging up on a cordless phone, I called her back.

"What are you going to do when you get here?" she asked.

"What do you mean?" I had no clue where this conversation was coming from. Recently our calls had been a little strained. We started to miss a day here and there. I blamed my frustration with how little progress I had made on the new novel. After every publisher to whom my agent sent my first novel had passed, my confidence in my writing wasn't at an all-time high.

When we met in graduate school, Meredith's and my shared passion for writing had felt like a belief in the same god. Despite this compatibility, we rarely talked to each other about our work. Opening up to her about the wall I had hit seemed like a positive development.

"We never fixed anything," she said.

On TV, Darrell Hammond was doing Bill Clinton in a *Saturday Night Live* rerun. I had muted it before calling, but left it on, the screen's flicker the only light inside the black tunnel in which I unexpectedly found myself. I stared in the TV's direction, but it was too far, five feet away, for my eyes to discern more than movement.

In an email the next day, Meredith apologized for calling after drinking most of a bottle of wine. Her apology didn't extend to the content of her words, only how bluntly she had said them. "I will not," she elaborated days later, "be complicit in your lie."

I wasn't sure which word hurt more, lie or the B-word embedded so thornily in the next line. *Blindness. Your blindness. I will not help you hide your blindness from the world.* She had never used that word around me before. If she knew how deeply it wounded me, would she have avoided it or moved it from quiver to bow years ago?

It's better and worse than you might imagine. This is what I'd like to tell people who ask about my eyesight. What most people want to know is what I see when I look at them, and the short answer is this: I don't see what I look directly at. If I look up or to the side, I can see something, and this usually fends off further questions. This answer allows people to imagine, however erroneously, that my blind spots are smudges on the center of a mirror from which I can escape by looking elsewhere on the mirror. Lies of omission weren't ones I hastened to correct.

Instead of a smudge, picture a kaleidoscope. Borderless shapes fall against each other, microscopic organisms, a time-lapsed photograph of a distant galaxy. Dull colors flicker and swirl: mustard yellow, pale green, magenta.

"That would drive me crazy," a friend once said when I described my blind spots for her.

The most frequent compliment heard by people with a disability is *I could never do what you do*, but everyone knows how to adapt. When it's cold outside, we put on a coat. When it rains, we grab an umbrella. A road ends, so we turn left, turn right, turn around. We adapt because it's all we can do when we cannot change our situation.

I can still see out of the corners of my eyes, but here's the thing about peripheral vision: The quality of what you see isn't the same as what you see head-on. Imagine a movie filmed with only extras, a meal cooked using nothing but herbs and a dash of salt, a sentence constructed only of metaphors. To see something in your peripheral vision with any acuity, it has to be quite large. On top of this, my periphery isn't unaffected by the blind spots.

Looking directly into a mirror, I am not without a face. My kaleidoscopic clouds permit enough light to see pronounced contrasts like my eyes, nostrils, the crease where my lips meet. Of the many mundane abilities my remaining sight permits me, I am especially grateful for the ability to feign eye contact, if not always as convincingly as I would prefer. The closer someone's face and the better the lighting, the more easily I can keep track of the shadows between nose and forehead. A few inches from the mirror, I can gauge with some accuracy if all the coffee I've consumed has stained my teeth, style my hair, ponder the accuracy of a girl who told me when I was twenty that I kind of looked like Ben Affleck, which might or might not have compelled me to defend the actor's sometimes-problematic career choices for the next two decades.

When our emails finally reverted back to phone calls after our argument, I asked the only question that seemed to matter: Should I move to Nashville? I had already given notice to my employer. For the past four months, I had slept on an air mattress and eaten off chipped plates I planned to donate to Goodwill.

Meredith's hesitation felt like an answer. She asked what I thought.

"I think your answer is more important than mine."

Another pause. "If you don't, this doesn't have much of a chance, does it?"

"That isn't a yes."

"Then yes."

It wasn't the starry tone with which she'd uttered that word when I slid an engagement ring around her finger, but it was better than no.

Meredith and I barely speak while we finish unloading the car. A Christmas cartoon blares on the TV. Meredith asks Mom if she wants to try the mulled wine. There's also pumpkin bread.

I step into the bathroom with my coat still on. The bathroom has two doors, one leading to the hall and one to the bedroom. I lock both of them and bury my face in a bath towel. After a few minutes, I pull myself together. How apparent will it be that I have been crying? I study the blurry face in the mirror. If I stare at things long enough, I like to tell people, they eventually come into focus, but this is not true.

1

ALL THE ANSWERS

THE FIRST HINTS ARE the half-erased words on the overhead projector. Most of your teachers recycle lesson plans, but from your seat in the last row of a high school lecture hall, Mrs. Jones's smudged transparencies seem aggressively lazy. You study the notebook of the guy beside you, who also squints at the screen. His notes could be charitably described as judicious, but they contain a number of lines you couldn't piece together.

You tell your mom you need glasses. She makes you an appointment with Dr. Keane, the optometrist who bears a striking resemblance to Chicago Bulls coach Phil Jackson. "Is Dead God?" asks an *Entertainment Weekly* cover in his waiting room, the question floating beside the disembodied head of Jerry Garcia. You turn pages, nonchalant about the prospect of reinventing your look. If you're being honest, the no-glasses look hasn't gotten you very far.

Dr. Keane sees right away what's wrong. When he covers your right eye, the eye chart disappears. He invites you and your mom into his office. He calls you a "monocular" patient. His receptionist makes you an appointment with another doctor. Dr. Keane doesn't seem worried.

Weeks later, you sit before a half-dome the size of a beach ball for your first visual field test. Resting your chin on a metal ledge, you fix your eyes, one at a time, on a tiny light in the center of the orb. In your hand is a buzzer like the ones held by *Jeopardy!* contestants. Tiny spotlights of varying size appear throughout the dome, and you press the button whenever you see one, if you see one. Lights slide like meteors across the sphere, vanquished by the buzzer.

According to the visual field, your right eye is fine. Your left, however, which your optometrist graded 20/400, has only peripheral vision.

A nurse seems pleased to inject dye into your bloodstream, a test for trauma she seldom gets to administer. Two ophthalmologists take turns peering into your pupils. When no trauma is detected, they shake your hand, a chess opponent they had underestimated.

They refer you to an optic nerve specialist at the university hospital in Morgantown. A Bea Arthur look-alike wearing a turtleneck beneath her lab coat, Dr. Ellis sees something is wrong with your optic nerve. If you had to put your medical fate in the hands of a Golden Girl, Dorothy would be your first choice.

Dr. Ellis orders an MRI and your day trip to Morgantown becomes an overnighter. Killing time, you and your parents tour the university you have no desire to attend. All the brochures you requested at the recent college fair were for schools in the neighboring states of Ohio, Pennsylvania, and Maryland, even one in California.

When the MRI shows nothing unusual, you prepare for Dr. Ellis to shake your hand. Instead, she offers a diagnosis: optic neuritis. A swelling of the optic nerve, it often goes away on its own. She orders an intravenous steroid treatment to expedite recovery.

With that settled, your thoughts turn to the other elephant in the room, at least from where you sit. "So I'm okay to drive?"

Dr. Ellis, without hesitation, says driving shouldn't be a problem.

Thank you for being a friend.

Few milestones embody the start of adulthood like the passing of one's driver's test. You passed yours on the first try, the day after your sixteenth birthday. Grateful shout-out to the state trooper who gave you three attempts at parallel parking.

Your excitement was surpassed only by your mom's consternation. Having your license doesn't mean you get to drive everywhere, she cautioned on the way home, but her warning rang a little hollow, coming from the passenger seat.

Only one of your close friends has ever had a girlfriend. It seems no coincidence that he's your only friend with a car. Another guy in school, who once sat by himself in the corner of the cafeteria and as far as you can tell has no friends at all, began dating the head majorette within weeks of obtaining his Mazda Miata. Hoping to chart a similar path, you linger for several minutes each morning after parking your pre-owned Mustang in the lot across from the school.

Having a car is a bit of a coup. In contrast to the wealthy neighborhoods surrounding your high school, you live on a dirt road where if it hasn't rained in a while the faucets cough out a muddy spray. Your parents got a deal on your Mustang from an uncle who owns a salvage lot.

More than once, you leave a book in the backseat so you can go back for it and let a new audience see you in all your car-unlocking, driver's-side-door-opening reverie. Leaving school in the afternoon, you make eye contact with as many girls as possible, looking for some change in how they see you. It's a process, you reassure yourself.

Spring break brings a three-day, three-night, all-expenses-paid (by insurance and your parents) stay in Charleston's St. Francis Hospital. It wasn't as though you had other plans. As you pack your pajamas and comic books, it feels a little like camping, if camping involved an adjustable bed, cable TV, and room service. Your private, carpeted room overlooks a tree-lined courtyard. The small TV is attached to a movable arm, allowing you to position it in front of your face, not that you need to. The vision in your right eye remains intact, and as long as you keep that eye open there's nothing wrong with you, something you have to remind your grandmother when she visits.

Once a day your neurologist, a friendly Indian American with a bald spot in his beard, stops by to examine your eyes. Dr. Nair reminds you of the cool senior on the tennis team who wears a diamond earring.

Your neurologist points to the wall, instructing you where to look, and peers through a magnifying glass into your left pupil. Because you told him during your spinal tap that you want to be a doctor, Dr. Nair carefully explains what he's looking for and how the optic nerves work.

"Have you noticed any changes?" he asks.

You close your right eye, blurring the room. "I don't think so."

It would be unusual to see results this quickly, he says. Despite his admonition, you check your left eye frequently, wondering how your vision will return. Will it be like a telescope coming into focus? Or will it return piece by piece, like a jigsaw puzzle?

Three afternoons of *Flipper* reruns come and go. Your parents bring your Easter basket to the hospital, but you can't eat the candy. The prednisone might cause bloating and, if you don't watch your sodium and calorie intake, weight gain. Thus, you return to school a little bloated, with one blurry eye, and braces still on your teeth for another year, but at least you have that car.

It's your first week back on the road, on the way to school, when a truck appears out of nowhere in the oncoming lane. You were in your own lane, and the truck was on its own side of the road, but where did it come from? You keep your eyes on the road in front of you, as one is supposed to do, as you had been doing. Your heart is still recovering from the sudden appearance of the truck when a station wagon zooms past you only a moment after you saw it.

From your second hospital bed in as many months, you try to follow the French Open on a wall-mounted TV. You can barely make out the red clay of Roland-Garros beside the pale green wall. After points and right before a serve, the camera zooms in on the faces of Mary Pierce and Mary Jo Fernández, but the points themselves you can only follow with your ears. One day you'll learn the difference between the pop of a volley and the click of a topspin lob, understand the time lapse between crosscourt ground strokes versus shots down the line, gauge the grace and difficulty of a return from the astonishment of spectators and TV commentators. Today you would settle for knowing which shots are in or out. The crowd seems to cheer harder for Mary Pierce, who is half French, but you don't understand the chair umpire, having taken Spanish for the last three years.

Within days of your good eye going the way of the bad one, Dr. Nair ordered another round of steroids. Due to availability, your room this time is in the pediatric ward of a hospital across town, much farther from home. The lack of carpet makes these quarters feel more like a hospital. When your grandmother visits, it's harder to shrug off her concern.

Optimism led you to bring your school books to the hospital for this second treatment. Whether you would have completed your homework, even if you could still read, is up for debate. In recent years, you've rarely found homework more enticing than *The Arsenio Hall Show* or *Saturday Night Live* reruns. In elementary school, batteries of tests with more positive results allowed you to skip an entire grade, but a lazy B average has steadily undermined that potential. Each time your grades dipped, first in junior high and again in high school, you weren't alarmed. After all, you remained a year younger than your peers. And don't grades only measure how hard you try?

A few times you open your history book, but the print is too small to read even with your nose touching the page. You've had to memorize the buttons on the remote control. Several times a day you stare at your hand, trying to decide if there's more or less of it than the day before. The first two mornings you're excited to open your eyes and check for improvements. Upon finding none, waking up becomes less appealing.

"How can you stay in here all day?" your dad asks, annoyed to find you in your pajamas at three in the afternoon.

"Where am I supposed to go?"

"Go for a walk," he says. "You don't have to stay in this damn room."

"What difference does it make?"

The answer, you realize, is that he prefers not to see you in a hospital bed. There isn't anything wrong with your body, nothing to prevent you from moving about, and seeing you in bed only reminds him that you are losing your sight. What he tells you, however, is that the medicine isn't going to work if you're lying around all day.

The next time Dr. Nair stops by, you ask him if this is true.

It isn't, he assures you, explaining the physiology of it all. You don't have the heart to tell this kind man that despite what you told him during your first visit, you've never really wanted to be a doctor. You began saying this back in elementary school, noticing how much it impressed grown-ups. Lately you're not sure what you want to be, what you can be, with the entire eye chart a shapeless blur. Gone is the bald spot in Dr. Nair's beard. Gone is his beard, his face. At this point, instead of letters, you're counting the number of fingers he holds up, and you can only guess.

Before your parents' next visit, you put on jeans and a T-shirt. You don't mention that you were right about the medicine. Your mom and dad have continued working a full day only to drive across town to the hospital, nothing to do once they get here but sit in a chair and watch you listen to the TV. They are as frustrated as you are when after three days and countless popsicles from the pediatric nurses, your vision is worse than when you were admitted.

Only two days remain in your junior year of high school. The bells have been turned off. Students with normal numbers of absences aren't required to attend. It isn't the number of days you've missed but final exams that make your presence mandatory.

Not one of your friends is in school. With everything going on, their finals and your latest hospital stay, you've hardly talked to any of them in over a week. Your friend with the car offered to visit you in the hospital, but you declined. It was only a few days. You'd see him soon enough.

With no one else to talk to, you sit with the Indian kid

other Indian kids tease for having a name both American and uncool. Let's call him Melvin. More than his name, Melvin is ostracized for never taking honors classes and barely pulling out B's and C's in his regular classes. Next year, when most of your friends become acquaintances and acquaintances strangers, you and Melvin will find yourselves killing time with each other in the library and office of your guidance counselor more days than not. Your two best friends will remain close, but you can no longer look for all the people with whom you used to sit in the library and cafeteria. After a month or two, they no longer look for you.

It feels strange, presenting your teachers with documentation of where you've been and what you cannot currently do. You never have been the doctor's note sort. For several years, you haven't been any sort, really, and you can't help wondering if this new difference might be the result of wishful thinking gone awry.

Your chemistry teacher, that subject not particularly compatible with an oral exam, lets you keep the C you are fortunate to still have after weeks of not seeing the chalk-scrawled equations. Ditto precalculus. You thought you had an outside shot at bringing your B in Spanish up to an A with a solid performance on the final, but the math shows otherwise. You forgo that final, too.

You rejoin Melvin in homeroom, nothing left to do but last the day. Melvin isn't even in your regular homeroom, but a few teachers have begun their summers a little early. Textbooks had been collected while you were gone. A custodian helps you open your locker, the combination too small for you to read. The clang of it closing echoes in the empty classrooms. The lights are off in so many of them it hardly feels like school.

TV has become radio. You find yourself watching a lot of stand-up comedy, game shows, CNN. Perhaps the information you retain will mask what you don't know—what you cannot know because you cannot see. Will people you meet question your intelligence? Blind, after all, is a common synonym for ignorant.

You memorize buttons on the microwave, track listings on all your CDs, heating instructions for your favorite frozen foods. You've always had a good memory. When you were younger, your parents refused to play Trivial Pursuit with you, saying you had memorized all the answers. You told them it wasn't cheating if the answers came from your own brain, that remembering was the same as knowing.

The blind spots continue to expand. Every day there's something new you can no longer see, another shelf of memory claimed by everyday tasks. How much space does your mental hard drive contain? In seventh grade, you finished a not-too-shabby third in the school spelling bee, competing against eighth and ninth graders, but yesterday you couldn't remember if monitor is spelled with an -or or an -er.

Six nights a week you schedule a date with *Jeopardy!* and Alex Trebek. Unlike in Trivial Pursuit, you don't need anyone to play with, and Trebek helpfully reads all the clues on the screen. You've always found the whole phrasing-answers-in-the-form-of-a-question thing kind of pretentious, but it's still questions and answers—questions that *have* answers.

Once in a while, you come upstairs to watch TV with your parents. After a recent argument, the distance between your bedroom and the living room, between you and your parents, feels greater than it used to. Weeks afterward, you no longer recall what was said, only that it made you cry, which made your mom cry, and after that nobody knew what to say.

Your dad changes the channel to *Jeopardy!*, a peace offering. Four categories in, your parents notice you've only missed one clue. Early in the Double Jeopardy round, you consider telling them it's a rerun, that you remember the answers from a prior airing, but you keep it to yourself. What they don't know won't hurt them.

2

LAND OF THE
RISING SUN

WEEKS AFTER MY DIAGNOSIS, we received a call from a Harvard researcher who specialized in my condition. Despite his upbeat tone, he agreed with the Johns Hopkins ophthalmologist who had put us in touch, that no treatment existed for Leber's hereditary optic neuropathy.

"Are you researching cures?" Mom asked when I passed her the phone.

"Yes and no," he said.

His research involved similar conditions, related mutations, information contained in the mitochondria. Rare as Leber's was, the race for a cure wasn't exactly a wind sprint.

"So there's absolutely nothing we can do," Mom said.

The researcher hesitated. In a few countries, he said, some doctors were using a drug they believed beneficial for Leber's patients. A twelve-year-old boy in Japan had been administered idebenone and experienced a full recovery of his lost vision. There remained some uncertainty, cautioned the researcher, about whether Leber's was actually what the boy had and whether idebenone was what caused his recovery.

"How do we order it?" Mom said.

Because idebenone had not been approved by the FDA, it could only be procured by visiting one of the countries he had named.

"If it was your son, would you go?" Mom had been talking with the researcher for nearly an hour. His young daughter, he had mentioned, was severely hearing-impaired and was about to undergo another in a series of experimental surgeries.

"I probably would," he said.

The idebenone-friendly doctor with whom the researcher was most familiar was the very one in Japan who had possibly cured the twelve-year-old boy. My parents priced plane and hotel fare with my uncle, the one who had helped us acquire my car. He had recently opened a travel agency, but even with his discount the cost was enormous. There must be cheaper hotels than the Tokyo Hilton, but his agents had never booked a trip to Asia. On top of travel, the doctor's visit and year's supply of idebenone wouldn't be covered by insurance.

Mom and Dad never mentioned in front of me how much my malady was costing them, but I had overheard some numbers. My parents had worked their way up from school custodian and secretary when I was born to jobs in purchasing for the school board and insurance sales. Since moving into my grandparents' old house when I was seven, they had been saving up to move into the city. Guilty as I felt, I raised no objections. If there was a one-in-a-thousand chance this drug could work, and no one gave us any numbers, my vote was for rolling the dice.

Mom and I would depart in mid-September, two weeks into my senior year. To save the cost of a third plane ticket, Dad would sit this one out. My teachers were excited for my adventure. We got to know one another quickly in light of all the accommodations I now required. The owner of my regular comic book shop gave me money to get her a T-shirt from Tokyo's Hard Rock Cafe. I still picked up new comics every Friday, hopeful that I might be able to read them again.

Mom and Dad met with the bank about converting dollars to yen. Doctors said there shouldn't be any complications with bringing the medicine back into the United States. The question of how we would get from Narita International Airport to downtown Tokyo, or from the Tokyo Hilton to Keio Hospital, armed with exactly three Japanese phrases—good morning, excuse me, and yes—remained unanswered. Also uncertain was my pronunciation and translation of these phrases, learning them as I had from an episode of *Designing Women*.

Our plane departed Charleston's Yeager Airport in the early evening, landing in Lexington, Kentucky, half an hour later. From there, we settled in at O'Hare for a five-hour layover before our eight-hour leg to Anchorage, Alaska. Two hours later, an eleven-hour jaunt delivered us to Seoul, from which point, after another two-hour layover, we finally touched down in Tokyo. We weren't surprised when my uncle's travel agency folded after only a year.

In her bolder, teenage years, my mother once climbed onstage at a Blood, Sweat & Tears concert to plant a kiss on the lead singer. Her sneaking out at night became a problem my grandfather solved by chaining the axle of her car to an oak tree. Responsible, traditional mother that she became, I wouldn't hear these stories until I was much older. Digging through her purse for our week-old passports, she was the same timid traveler as her son, whose sixteen years had taken him no farther than his grandparents' trailer park in central Florida.

Gomennasai—excuse me—we found ourselves saying to everyone we spoke to, beginning with a cashier at an airport concession stand. Mom read me the price in yen for two Diet Cokes, and in my head I calculated how much we were actually paying. Eight dollars. The only drinks Korean Air offered were warm soda and warm juice. We didn't know the word for thank you, so we smiled big and hoped everyone understood our gratitude.

In second grade, we moved from an apartment in the city into the rural house where Mom had grown up. Right outside city limits, the unincorporated area was marked by lush forest, creeks at the bottom of hills, and a lot of dirt roads. That there was anything inferior about an address with a route number instead of a street name didn't occur to me until seventh grade. Social lines at John Adams Junior High were drawn between kids from "the creek" and kids from South Hills, like something out of S. E. Hinton.

Whether it was the school bus I rode, not knowing anyone in any of my honors classes, or my Levi's coming from
the shelf marked *husky*, my modest popularity in elementary
school didn't make the leap to junior high. Not yet aware of
this, I pulled on my best Bugle Boys and snazziest Alex P.
Keaton sweater and asked my parents for a ride to the autumn
dance. Egged on by a friend, I let him ask my crush if she
would dance with me. He returned with a broad smile. She
had accepted.

Annie Abadopolis was in six of my seven classes, the first
name on every roll. She had a short, Sheena Easton haircut
and a way of teasing our world geography teacher that made
her seem more like his peer than our fellow student. As far
as I could tell, she had no boyfriend—until we found each
other near the free throw line and I placed my hands around
her waist. Annie rested her hands on my shoulders, and we
swayed from side to side for all four minutes of "Never Tear
Us Apart." We only danced the one dance, but we didn't dance
with anyone else.

All weekend I wondered how it would work: Would we
rendezvous at each other's lockers between classes? Before the
first bell? Would a mutual friend smuggle a note between us
to clarify our new status? How it worked, it turned out, was
that we would dance our dance and never speak a word of it,
or to each other, for the balance of junior high.

My seventh-grade yearbook picture doesn't show a fat
kid, to the extent one can tell from the head and shoulders.
Aware that the waist size of my jeans was larger than that
of other kids my height—thanks, Levi Strauss, for stamping

those black numbers on the outside of your jeans—I flouted the tucked-in trend to hide those gaudy integers. A glance at my eighth-grade yearbook, however, shows the emergence of a double chin. Thank you as well to my hometown's answer to Annie Leibovitz for managing to capture my entire torso, my windbreaker cascading toward the picture's lower border in a manner reminiscent of a muumuu.

A year earlier, Mom had joined Weight Watchers and easily lost her goal weight of fifteen pounds. Nothing sounded worse than attending her weekly meetings, looking on while women exchanged soup recipes, but maybe I didn't have to. I already understood how to measure foods into what the program called exchanges. Most meals Dad cooked were Weight Watchers friendly, and I had come to prefer the diet sodas we had been drinking for years.

I told no one I was dieting. Telling people you're trying to lose weight only underscores that weight needs to be lost. One day in the Taco Bell drive-through, while Mom calculated the Weight Watchers value of a bean burrito, I provided the answer a little too quickly. I was known in the family for having a quick memory, but Mom did a double take.

"I'm keeping track of what I eat," I confessed.

My diet continued with Mom's assistance. For lunch, I made sandwiches with low-fat meat, low-fat cheese, mustard instead of mayo, on 35-calorie wheat bread with more air pockets than a cheap sponge. I filled Ziploc bags with celery and carrot sticks—unlimited foods—and a recycled yogurt container filled with applesauce. Rather than a svelte appearance in my husky jeans, the biggest result was ravenous hunger after lunch and dinner. Still dining several times a week at Taco Bell, I might have strayed from the core tenets of the Weight Watchers plan. Nor did it help that my only exercise was thumb aerobics of up-up-down-down-left-right-left-right-B-A-start on a Nintendo controller. According to the scales, two months of dieting had taken off between four and six pounds.

By tenth grade, I had given up on dieting, though I continued to count fat grams. The fourteen-year-old looking back at me in the mirror had a narrower face and, if I tilted my neck at a slight upward angle, only one chin. The changes came less from dietary choices than a small growth spurt. Nor did it hurt that I tagged along with my parents to the YMCA as they took up tennis. I was far from thin, but I finally managed enough confidence to tuck my shirts into those sky-blue Levi's. To my daily disappointment, despite my sartorial adjustments, my popularity didn't budge.

Being a teenage boy without self-confidence or a girlfriend placed me squarely in the majority of my age bracket, which didn't make me feel any less alone. The teenage years are an interminable parade of *someday* and *soon*, hour after hour of wishing you could fast-forward to life's good parts. I was ready for a change, ready to be changed, but the loss of my sight a month after turning sixteen wasn't what I had in mind.

I had moved from the car's driver's seat back to the passenger side. I had begun reading textbooks with my ears instead of my eyes. I adjusted my career plans from doctor to the more modest, less vision-dependent physical therapist. Soon I would rethink my enrollment at West Virginia University, the giant school most of my friends were attending.

———

People in Tokyo who didn't speak some English were rare. Even the less proficient, when we *gomennasai*'d them on the street, mustered a perfectly enunciated "I do not speak English." Noticing our confusion by the subway ticket machine, a man in a baseball cap gave us tickets from his pocket. We tried to pay him, and he waved us off with a smile.

The Japanese-English dictionary we had bought from Waldenbooks was no help with the Japanese characters on signs and menus. We hadn't bothered with guidebooks or sightseeing recommendations, but we saw plenty, much of it several times over as lunches and dinners became hours-long expeditions. At one point, we ascended a subway escalator to find ourselves on the fourth floor of a department store that seemed to sell nothing but kimonos.

Street smells alternated between frying meat and curb-side garbage, both odors intensified by the summer heat. We walked for miles and miles, calves burning, blisters forming on the pads of my feet. We were lost even when we knew where we were.

The morning of my doctor's appointment, Mom tried to make heads or tails of the machine that dispensed subway and train tickets. I wished the man in the baseball cap had shown us how to use the machine instead of giving us his tickets. My disability only a few months old, I hadn't yet learned the difference between good help and bad.

At last a transit worker assisted us with the machine, and we followed the crowd to the platform. Within minutes we were surrounded inside the train by dozens of commuters, bodies pushing against bodies. For a long moment the doors wouldn't close. I folded my arms, making room.

I listened to the garbled voice in the speakers for the name of our stop. When I heard it, I told Mom.

Our heads turned toward the opening doors. They were the only body parts we could move.

"Excuse us," Mom said.

"*Gomennasai*," I said.

"*Gomennasai*," Mom said.

We made it six inches closer to the doors before they closed.

A few passengers got off at the next stop, replaced immediately by new passengers. My appointment drew closer, the hospital getting farther away.

Four stops too late, we were able to squeeze our way off the train. On the bright side, the train hadn't seemed to go far between stops. On the dim side, we couldn't tell, after reaching the street, which direction the train had taken us.

We asked someone where we were. It didn't go well. We asked someone else. He seemed as confused by our map as we were and apologized in English. Being the one who could see the map, Mom did the talking. We spoke the hospital's name to people we passed. Some smiled and shook their heads. Finally, a man pointed us in the direction we were already walking.

Eight, nine, ten blocks later, we had yet to come to a structure large enough to be a hospital. Buildings no longer had signs. Was this a residential neighborhood? We had been the only people on the sidewalk for some time. Certainly buses went to the hospital, but how would we know which one?

Would a taxi driver know which hospital we meant? Not that we had seen a bus or taxi in over an hour.

Mom checked her watch every few minutes. We had two appointments, one in the morning and another in the afternoon. Two hours had gone by since we left the hotel, and we couldn't say if we were any closer to the hospital.

Then there it was. The tall, hospital-sized building appeared before us more suddenly than tall buildings tend to appear. We remained skeptical until we were upon it, until Mom could read the Roman letters on the sign by the entrance.

It was a new experience but a familiar feeling. My life had become a search for a skyscraper down a series of foreign streets, the letters on signs bearing no resemblance to the alphabet I had always known. But a hospital was still a hospital: automatic doors, people in white coats walking purposefully toward elevators, the same sterile smell as in every other hospital I had ever been inside. Everything remained the same, I told myself, even if I couldn't see it.

Maria Patel had been in my grade since junior high, but senior year was the first time we had classes together. Some of her friends occasionally hung out with some of my friends. A fellow senior with a bubbly laugh and a taste for long, floral skirts, Maria might not have known my name prior to this year, and she seemed justifiably surprised to find me calling her one evening in early November.

The conversation went well. English teachers told me I was witty, and Maria Patel was among the students who laughed at my little quips in class. She hesitated only slightly before accepting my offer to get dinner and see the Charleston Light Opera Guild's production of *My Fair Lady*.

I had my parents drop me off at the Charleston Town Center mall around five. "Some people are going to this play thing," I told them, letting Mom and Dad believe I was meeting the guys for an evening of musical theater, as sixteen-year-old guys did all the time in West Virginia circa 1993. I wasn't even sure it was a date. I didn't know what else it might be, but wishes don't come true if you tell people what you wished for.

I had spent more hours of my life in the mall than anywhere other than home or school. Monday nights after dinner, Mom cold-called from her office two blocks away, and I'd wander my favorite stores until closing time. Today, navigating the concourse by memory, I felt like George Bailey in *It's a Wonderful Life*, after he wishes he were never born and Bedford Falls is still Bedford Falls but somehow not the Bedford Falls he has always known.

For the first time since losing my sight, I navigated the aisles of Waldenbooks, where I had spent so many hours over the years they could have charged me rent. Holding a few hardcovers close enough to decipher the titles, I ran my thumb across the puffy lettering. In Camelot Music, remembering the location of genres, I deduced where I was from the first album cover I recognized. Weeks later, I would buy an Eagles CD I didn't particularly want just to remember what it felt like to buy something I found without any help.

But buying things never had been the point of the mall. Its pleasures lay in exploring racks and shelves, in imagining near and distant futures in the ever-changing contents of store windows. Now the entire mall seemed trapped behind a store window, the glass frosted over. "You are here," claimed the mall directories, but here was somewhere else.

Exiting through Montgomery Ward, I braced myself for my first solo mission as a legally blind pedestrian. On the dirt road where we lived, the only places to walk were the mailbox and my grandparents' house. Walking indoors, in school and stores and living rooms, was largely fine. Aiming my gaze directly in front of me, I had a partial view of where I was going, if not where I was. It's the matter of traffic that makes walking outdoors more complicated.

My parents hadn't seemed concerned about me crossing streets. Then again, I had told them I was meeting friends at the mall. Approaching the crosswalk, I regretted not suggesting one of the restaurants in the Town Center. The darkening sky provided enough contrast to see the traffic lights change from red to green. Stopped cars also let me know when to cross.

I arrived at Rio Grande very early, making sure Maria would have to spot me instead of the other way around. I had chosen a restaurant with which I was familiar. Strange environs weren't impossible, but it seemed a good idea to avoid any chance of poor lighting, a gauntlet of tightly arrayed tables, sudden steps up or down, or waiting in the foyer of the wrong restaurant.

My heart raced each time the door opened. If it was two or more people, I could infer it was not Maria. Guys by themselves were not Maria. Women without black hair who were not a head shorter than me were not Maria. Within a few minutes she would step through the door and I would have no trouble recognizing her—she was the one who paused in front of me and said "Hey J.T."—but self-doubt is a bottomless basket of chips to a legally blind sixteen-year-old on the first date of his life.

Maria scanned the menu, and I pretended to do the same. If she was aware of my low vision, she didn't let on. I certainly hadn't told her. The possibility of a mutual friend having mentioned it made me queasy.

It wasn't only that I refused to identify as blind. I wasn't blind. I could still see things. And every day that I passed for the fully sighted person I used to be made it easier to believe there was nothing wrong.

Dr. Tanaka's intern, whose proficiency with English was much better than his superior's, escorted us from floor to floor. They drew my blood, took vitals, gave me a standard eye exam and a visual field test. The visual field test was my first since the one I had taken at Johns Hopkins in June. Since then, my blind spots had continued to expand. Doctors said my acuity would level off between 20/200 and 20/400. I still had faith in doctors, in medicine, despite how many had misdiagnosed what I had. Traveling to another continent for expensive, experimental pills that might or might not have restored the vision of a twelve-year-old boy who *possibly* had the same condition I had was nothing if not an act of faith.

Dr. Tanaka's intern walked us to the hospital's restaurant, where Mom described pictures on the menu. My magnifiers, only two months old, were already ineffective for reading most menus. The arrival of forks with our entrées was a welcome change from the chopsticks that had confounded our fingers for the last forty-eight hours.

At my afternoon appointment, Dr. Tanaka greeted us with silent handshakes. He didn't possess the English for small talk. I had a seat in the examining chair. When Dr. Tanaka peered into my eyes, part of me expected him to see something all my American doctors had missed. Crossing an ocean has a way of inflating expectations.

Dr. Tanaka invited his intern to have a look—my eyes were quite educational, I had come to realize. They conferred briefly in Japanese while we filled out paperwork.

Suddenly we were all shaking hands. Final stop: the hospital pharmacy. A year's supply of idebenone filled a box no larger than a clock radio. Medicine in hand, we found a waiting area with seats and tore into the plastic. They were round white pills the size of Advil. One sheet held twenty-one pills, or a week's worth. I pushed one through the foil backing and held it in my fist while we searched for a water fountain.

Maria and I flipped through our programs, having exhausted topics of conversation. A couple of times she pointed wordlessly to what I assumed was a photograph. I responded with an all-purpose smile. At last the houselights went off. All eyes turned to the stage. Dark as it was, I felt confident no one would see mine were aimed at the proscenium.

I had been taking the little white pills for two months. If I noticed changes, Dr. Tanaka said, they would likely be gradual. In the back of my head, however, flashed the phrase *spontaneous recovery*, the words doctors had used to describe the effects of the drug on that twelve-year-old boy. I tested my eyes frequently, fixing my gaze on the glass dome of my bedroom ceiling fan, tracking how much of each blade I could still see. Not since stepping on my grandmother's scales during junior high had I paid so much attention to my body. For nearly a year, going back to the pair of steroid treatments and the incorrect diagnosis of optic neuritis, I had been watching the ceiling fan disappear.

"Give it time," said the pastor at the church we had attended when I was younger. We stopped going when I was ten or eleven, for no reason that I could remember. Now my parents and I found ourselves in the pew every Sunday. I wasn't sure if I still believed in God. I thought I did. I wanted to think I did, but the inclusion of my name in the weekly prayer bulletin wasn't making a difference.

The first blind person I ever met went to our church. He was still there when we returned. Born without sight, he used a cane and never opened his eyes. Possibly they didn't open. He had a singing voice like Donny Osmond and once a year sang "The Man from Galilee" during the service. When Mom told him I was losing my sight, he was one of the few who didn't say he'd pray for me.

"Hang in there," he said and shook my hand.

After a few weeks of the pills, I did notice subtle differences. In brighter rooms, when I closed my eyes a few patches of my eyelids registered as bright red. There seemed to be a small, hazy window in the blind spot of my right eye. If

I stared long enough at a paragraph of text, the letters of a single word almost came into partial focus. A year later, this would remain the only change in my vision, but for months, if I squinted hard enough, uncertainty looked a lot like hope.

On the lighted stage in the dark theater, costumed figures danced and sang. The frequency with which people laughed made me wonder if I was missing some physical comedy. None of the dialogue struck me as particularly funny. In fairness to Lerner and Loewe, all I could focus on throughout the first act was whether I should make a move.

I couldn't muster the confidence to slip my arm around Maria. She had given no indication that this gesture would precipitate a tilt of her head onto my shoulder. The armrest between us had yet to be used by her or me. The only other move I could think of was holding her hand. That much I had done before, on sixth-grade field trips with Julie Schiffman. Back then I had the confidence of having been told, through no less credible a source than Julie's sister, that Julie liked me first. Who was to say how things were going with Maria? The only way I could think to offer her my hand without grabbing hers was setting my hand on my leg, palm up, and waiting for her to take it.

Intermission came and went. The curtain rose again, and I returned my hand to the same spot near my knee. Even if she saw it there, I worried Maria wouldn't realize I was offering it to her. I wiggled my fingers. No dice. Each time the stage went dark, I feared it was all over, but the lights kept coming back on. Another song. Another scene. It was a long show.

3

REAL BOOKS

I NEVER HAD BEEN much of a reader. In elementary school, the wobbly stacks of library books I carried past clown murals every Saturday consisted of how-to-draw manuals, guides for making paper airplanes, and photo galleries of old monster movies. Occasionally, when book reports forced my hand, I managed to get lost in a short novel, but the only non-illustrated books I read of my own volition were entries in the *Choose Your Own Adventure* series. And yes, I was a *Choose Your Own Adventure* cheater. Given the options at the end of a chapter, *to do this, go to this page* or *to do that, go to that page*, I peeked to see which involved less text. Eventually, I made the logical leap to comic books and never looked back, until the burnout of my optic nerves rendered every panel of *Sandman* and *Hellblazer* as abstract as a Jackson Pollock.

Following the diagnosis of Leber's, I met with a low vision specialist to discuss adaptive aids. My vision was uncorrectable, so reading meant making words large enough to skirt my central blind spots. The low vision doctor looked like Molly Ringwald's bookish sister. That's who I pictured, anyway. In the month since the diagnosis, faces had become suggestions of faces, shaped in my mind by someone's voice and personality.

Dr. Ringwald handed me magnifiers and pages with text. Right away we moved past the wide, Sherlock Holmes style with a handle. The only models that allowed me to read fonts in a magazine—a few words at a time—were the three-inch-tall loupes I had only seen in movies. Think jewel thieves scrutinizing diamonds for subtle imperfections.

"How much does this one cost?" I asked, wondering if insurance would pay for these devices.

"Don't tell him how much anything costs," Dad said.

The doctor, smiling, said her policy was not to hide any information from the patient. She revealed the exorbitant price of everything she handed me. My parents, somewhat testily, made it clear to me that price wasn't an issue.

"Speaking of prices," the doctor said, "I want you to tell me how much that says."

She handed me a rectangular price tag you'd find on a new sweater. I placed the 15× loupe against it and told her the listed price.

"Are you sure about that?"

I returned the magnifier to the bottom of the tag, making sure I had not mistaken an eight for a nine or a six. The numbers still looked like the ones I thought I had seen. The doctor asked if I saw anything unusual near the bottom. A thin, light red line ran the length of it. To the left of the red line was a handwritten number. It was a disheartening lesson: Even when I saw *something*, I might not see *everything*.

I left with four different magnifiers, a four-inch telescope I could theoretically use to see the chalkboard or overhead projections, a plastic holder into which you could slide checks to keep everything on the right lines, and a ream of special notebook paper. The latter had black lines with plenty of space between them, like the paper in elementary school for practicing cursive.

Dr. Ringwald signed paperwork to verify I was legally blind. One form granted me access to a specialized library for the blind and physically handicapped. The branch serving all of West Virginia was located in the Capitol Complex, a few miles from where we lived. A sign inside the Cultural Center led us to the basement. Somewhere in this building was the famed Mountain Stage, which R.E.M. once called one of their favorite venues, but the long, dim hallway where we ended up was less rock concert than abandoned radio station.

Inside, the odor of plastic was so thick it could have been a doll factory. I squinted in the bright fluorescent lights. When an older woman noticed us by the door, she assumed we were in the wrong place until Mom showed her my paperwork. Suddenly she was glad to see us.

In a brief tour, the librarian walked us down aisles of metal shelves, pointing to a stack of relics from the years when books were recorded on vinyl rather than cassettes. Most patrons being print-disabled, the library wasn't set up for browsing.

Instead, requests were made over the phone, and books were shipped for free through the mail. To return them, you simply flipped the postage label to the side with the library's return address, *Free Matter for the Blind* printed in the corner where postage would go.

The plastic scent in the air came from the pale green cartons that held the tapes. A second librarian emerged from a storage room with the special cassette player I would need to listen to books I checked out. Weighing around ten pounds, it was twice the size of my biggest textbook. All the cassettes held four sides, and the second librarian explained how to toggle between tracks one–two and tracks three–four. Another switch adjusted the vocal speed, from a frog's croak to Alvin and the Chipmunks on cocaine.

I thought we were here to check out school textbooks, but the first librarian said that a place called Recordings for the Blind handled those. The books here were the sort found in a regular library. When she asked if there was anything I wanted to check out, the question caught me off guard.

In the 1870s, Thomas Edison recorded the first audiobook, "Mary Had a Little Lamb," on the phonograph he invented. In the future, he believed, this would be the primary way people enjoyed books. Half a century would go by before technology allowed for longer recordings. Around that time, an act of Congress established the Talking Books program, which provided millions of visually impaired Americans access to the written word. By the 1990s, its collection was exponentially bigger than the books-on-tape section of a public library, still dominated by self-help titles, but it generally took best sellers a year to reach shelves. Mid-list titles that didn't win literary prizes seldom got recorded, but for the print-disabled who didn't know Braille, the Talking Books program was the only game in town.

I couldn't remember the last book I had read that wasn't assigned by an English teacher. Most of those I abandoned after twenty or thirty pages, piecing the rest together from class discussions and Cliffs Notes.

"Do you have *Jaws?*" I asked.

The librarian confirmed they had Peter Benchley's shark novel that became the Spielberg movie I had seen a dozen times. I asked if they had *Deliverance*. A further limitation of the library was that patrons needed to know what they wanted. Librarians would do their best in the coming years to correct my spelling of authors' names, but stumbling upon titles I didn't already know wasn't in the cards.

The librarian returned with the green cartons containing my selections. I wasn't convinced I was going to read them, but it felt good to have the option, to ask someone if I could do something and, for the first time in months, hear *yes*.

In my previous life as an ordinary teen, my after-school routine had been some combination of TV, Sega Genesis, napping, and reading comments on the Prodigy message boards. In light of ocular events, only television and sleep remained in the mix. For a few weeks after the diagnosis, I could still bring my face close enough to the computer to read brief messages, but an acuity of 20/70 in my good eye soon became 20/200 and falling. Holding a magnifier against the computer screen until the pixelated words came into focus proved tedious and eventually impossible.

As for watching TV, if I got close enough to the set, portions of the picture were large enough for me to follow what was happening. Seated on the foot of my bed, a few feet from the twenty-seven-inch TV, I found my ears were able to reconstruct most of the picture that I couldn't see.

The small telescope we had purchased from the low vision clinic justified its hefty price when I grew tired of sitting at the foot of my bed. I didn't dare pull it out in class, not only because it didn't make the writing on the overhead readable but because I wasn't about to out myself to any classmates not yet aware I was legally blind. Lying on my bed, I held the telescope to my better eye and aimed it at the TV. When my arm became tired, I shifted it to my other hand. Enlarging the screen didn't make it any clearer, so when both arms were tired I set the telescope on my nightstand. What I came to find, in these minutes when the blurry picture reverted to dancing light, was how well imagination replaced the picture.

It would be disingenuous to suggest watching movies and television wasn't significantly altered by the loss of my sight. The reason they call them movies, after all, is the same reason television surpassed radio in popularity. For every interchangeable car or sunrise, there are countless images we can behold a million times and never tire of seeing: the ocean, kittens, the naked body, one of those Hollywood smiles you feel in the pit of your stomach. The visual cues and cinematic grandeur I don't notice in a film's twenty-four frames per second could fill the shelves of a library, but I was surprised, despite what I couldn't see, how much of the story remained intact. Gradually I discovered that watching movies and TV with my ears felt a lot like reading.

"This book contains up to four sides per cassette. Side one: *Stories of Jack London* by Jack London. Narrated by John Stratton. Introduction by I. Milo Shepard. Approximate reading time: thirty-four hours and forty-six minutes. To skip past any prefatory material, press fast-forward until a beep is heard. At that point, press play for the table of contents or fast-forward until another beep is heard to hear the beginning of the book. Library of Congress annotation: Celebrated author of the Klondike . . ."

Listening to my first book on tape, a vague picture of the narrator popped into my head, the way one imagines the faces of people on the phone or radio. He sounded slender, perhaps a man in his late forties with thinning hair that has begun to gray. It's not as hard as you'd think to guess someone's appearance from their voice, inflection, and the personality that peeks around the corners of words. Minutes into the book, however, I was no longer picturing the narrator. Not long into the first story, the author's words became louder than the voice reading them.

On my way out of the library for the blind that first day, brainstorming other books I might check out, I had remembered enjoying the short story "To Build a Fire" in eighth grade, the only thing in a textbook I ever read by choice. Now I was listening to a story called "Love of Life," about a lost man on the verge of starvation in the Alaskan wilderness. In another, an Irish mother, out of stubbornness or resignation, gives each of her sons the same name, which seems to curse them to an early death. You could skip stories by fast-forwarding until the beep, but I never did. Within a few days, I had finished the entire book. Days after that, I finished another.

Over the years, people have asked if I noticed a difference between books on tape and reading print, and the answer is I don't know. Sporadic reader that I had been, it's hard to say if the words I read with my ears reached my brain differently than everything I had read with my eyes. For every study that shows comparably complex brain activity during both methods of reading, there's a respected author or literary critic who discredits audiobooks as more akin to watching television. Given my own seamless transition from watching TV with my ears to reading talking books, I'm in no position to refute such comparisons.

What I know for sure is this: Sooner or later, the voice in my ears ceases to be a voice. It becomes the words, the words become sentences, and the sentences become the story. At some point, the voice in my ears merges with my own voice the way the words on a page once became my own inner voice when I still read print. This happens less consciously when listening to professional narrators. Other times, with the less polished volunteers who recorded my textbooks or, years later, the digital voice of screen-reading software, the translation to an inner voice requires some effort.

In an unexpected development, perhaps the first pleasant alteration to my lifestyle in the wake of my first failed eye exam, I became a reader. Me. Books. One after another. In school, the kids who read books not assigned by an English teacher were what we called nerds. My friends and I were also nerds for collecting comic books, for never having girl-friends or weekend plans, but a handful of kids still stood out for seeming to live in their own world, tucked into a corner of the library with noses buried in an Isaac Asimov paper-back. One guy in my homeroom read while he walked, bump-ing into people like some caricature of a misfit from a John Hughes movie.

It wasn't fear of nerddom that kept me from reading dur-ing school hours. Even if I stowed the bulky cassette player in my backpack, there was no hiding my earphones. Not that there was anything wrong with earphones, but what if some-one asked what I was listening to? My answer would lead to another question, and another one after that. I hadn't intended my low vision to be a secret until I noticed the way some people, the ones who knew, now regarded me. Aside from my two best friends, people seemed to speak only to those around me. Thus, I did my reading at home, after school, usually with the lights off and the TV on mute.

My new reading life extended to my textbooks. For years I had done little more than skim assigned chapters, but staying on top of the reading for my classes meant one less thing I had to fake. As a result, most of my grades improved.

But was I actually reading? I regarded myself as a reader, but were these really books? Many years before I would think of myself as a writer, I was aware of the stigma associated with books on tape. Jokes on sitcoms implied audiobooks were to physical books what flag football is to the NFL. To read is to analyze, to study, to process information, and yet a tiny lump in the shape of a lie surfaced each time I used this verb to refer to titles I checked out from my special library.

Throughout college, after declaring an English major, I would clarify to friends that narrators of my audiobooks didn't *perform* what they read, as though a straightforward narration had more integrity, a closer relationship to the hardcovers sold in bookstores.

There is nothing quite like the scent of a book. The aroma of old paper when you enter a library is the smell of thought itself, of memory and time. For years, I would buy used books I could display on a shelf because being an English major and aspiring writer who didn't own books made me feel like more of an impostor than I already did. Occasionally I loaned them to people, letting the recipient assume that this copy I was giving them, this paperback or hardcover and not the four-track cassettes in the green plastic container, was the one I had read.

Occasionally, when no one was around, I would pull a book from the shelf and turn the pages. Even without a magnifier, my eyes can tell where the text lies, locate the little black wings on the otherwise blank page that must be the dedication. A few times I would hold the hardcover in my hand while the cassette played, guessing when to turn the page. I've feared I might be missing some element of the reading experience, that I might never have been reading at all. I worried that the short stories I wrote were not organic, authentic creations because all the books that inspired and educated me were consumed through secondary media, replications of the original text. A scholar of the humanities might point out the Homeric tradition of oral storytellers, noting that once upon a time writing and publishing didn't even exist. A few times I tried to write such an essay, defending the way I read by describing the different languages of the world, the unique alphabets with their own characters incomprehensible to other cultures. But there is no defense quite like the feeling that you have nothing to defend.

If the distinction between reading and listening didn't matter in the days of Homer, it mattered each time my freshman philosophy professor failed to remember our conversation about my eyes on the first day of class, when he continued to call on me to read aloud a passage of Sartre or Descartes and I had to announce my disability to a room of twenty-five college students I didn't know. It mattered in my dorm rooms when I stowed the white boxes of my recorded textbooks under my bed, stamped in black ink with *Recordings for the Blind* and *Free Matter for the Blind*. It mattered when, encountering Descartes in another class, the renowned philosopher declared sight "the noblest and most comprehensive of the five senses."

Alone in my bedroom at age sixteen, popping tape after tape into my talking book player, it didn't matter if I was reading or listening. The book titles on the side of the green cartons were the same as the copies found on the shelves of bookstores and regular libraries. They were the same authors. The words in my ears were the same words others saw when they held a book in their hands.

4
PASS/FAIL

THE DIRECTOR OF DISABILITY services welcomed us into his office with a smile and a moist handshake. My parents scheduled the appointment to discuss my transition from high school to the giant state university I planned to attend in the fall. Less than a year had gone by since the permanent burnout of my optic nerves. I wasn't a big fan of the label *legally blind*, but that's what I was. The word *disability*, no less accurate, seemed even worse.

"Do you know . . ." The man whose palm sweat I had furtively wiped on my jeans searched for my name in the papers in front of him. Not finding it, he asked me what it was.

I told him my name.

"Do you know, J.T., what's the best Christmas present you can give Mom and Dad your first semester of college?"

I said I did not.

"The best gift that first semester is a report card of all C's."

My parents and I stared blankly across the desk. I couldn't see their faces, but I could guess their expressions. As it happened, I had given them a similar present a couple of years ago, and they would have been grateful for the gift receipt.

"College is a hard adjustment," the director said. "Once you have that first semester under your belt, then you can start thinking about B's. Maybe even some A's."

"Which dorm should he stay in?" Mom asked, changing the subject. To my parents, despite my underwhelming B average, I remained the prodigy from elementary school who had been declared gifted and moved ahead a grade.

"Our blind students stay in the downtown dorms. That way they're just a short walk from us. Plus, most of his classes will be on this side of campus."

I cringed at his use of the B-word. It felt like a slur. Strictly speaking, I wasn't blind. I had my peripheral vision, fuzzy though it was. My eye condition—that's what it was, a condition, not a disability—might have put an end to my unremarkable driving career after two months, my pre-owned Mustang still awaiting sale in the Foodland parking lot, but I got around okay on foot. In New York City, most people didn't drive. I wasn't blind; I was a New Yorker.

It was a quiet car ride back to Charleston. Children without siblings come in two varieties: those who cope with the loneliness by learning how to befriend people, and those who befriend the silence. I was the latter. In my experience, expressing my feelings wasn't particularly effective in changing said feelings.

After twenty minutes on I-79, Mom finally spoke. "I'm sorry, but you're not a C student."

Dad let loose with a few R-rated words for the dean of low expectations. Mom noted how pleased with himself the man had seemed when he showed us his hearing aid, proof that he had overcome a disability. In truth, his approach to student success bothered me less than the prospect of staying in the downtown dorms. All my high school friends would be residing in the more modern towers on the other side of campus. They had already mailed their room deposits. Who was I going to eat meals with? Hang out with?

Farther down the road, out of the blue, Dad said, "That's supposed to be a good school, isn't it?"

Mom said the son of someone I didn't know went there. She named the college they must have seen advertised on a sign or billboard.

"What do you think?" Dad asked me. "Want to stop off and look around?"

My parents had taken some college classes after high school but opted for full-time jobs over completing their degrees. They didn't care where I attended college, only that I did. A year ago, I hadn't wanted to attend the university we just left. Now that I wouldn't be rooming with people I knew, what difference did it make where I went?

Minutes later, we were exiting the interstate, searching for a college to which I hadn't even applied. Mom and Dad narrated as we passed a video store, McDonald's, a Foodland the size of a pharmacy. Their descriptions of houses on the edge of campus betrayed an enthusiasm I couldn't muster. Somehow I doubted, and would later be disappointed to confirm, that the town of Buckhannon, West Virginia, population six thousand, was too small to have a Taco Bell.

A smiling woman in the admissions office couldn't have been happier to hear we had no appointment. She led us to the office of an admissions counselor, who was also glad to see us. No, it wasn't too late to apply for the fall semester.

In light of how the morning had gone, we dispensed with petty matters like academics and campus life, debriefing the admissions counselor on the nature of my impairment and what kind of accommodations I would need. Thanks to the Americans with Disabilities Act of a few years ago, any school would have to provide whatever I needed. It was the discretion with which said accommodations might be provided that most concerned me.

A peppy sophomore named Chris escorted us to a building across campus, where someone could answer the rest of our questions. As few buildings as there were, it wasn't hard to tell them apart. A girl exiting the library said Chris's name and he waved. I could do that, I thought: listen for my name and wave in the general direction from which it came.

Occupying the third floor of a normal-looking building, the Learning Center primarily assisted students with learning differences, but also helped students with physical limitations. Could I take my tests orally? Of course, said the director, an elderly, hunchbacked woman who, unlike the man from this morning, spoke to me rather than my parents. Could a reader record handouts or textbooks I couldn't obtain on tape? Absolutely. An attendant in the computer lab could open up a file, and when I was done typing a paper, someone from the writing center down the hall could make sure I had typed what I meant to type. If I paid frequent visits to this building, I wanted to ask, do you think I could pass for someone with a learning disability rather than a physical one? In fact, didn't you say the first floor housed the history and sociology departments? Could I pass for a history major?

The timing of my diagnosis gave me a year to adapt before college. Most importantly, it let me get out in front of the story, as the publicists say. I auditioned euphemisms for *legally blind*, my favorites being "bad eyes" and "vision problem." I liked the former for its air of blasé, the latter for its ambiguity.

Should anyone ever ask a follow-up—what's a vision problem? was a popular query—I named the two most significant activities I could no longer do: reading and driving. If other, countless activities might also present difficulty to someone for whom reading and driving are a problem, let's consider the inclusion of those activities implied and save us both a lot of time.

"I get my textbooks on tape," I told my freshman-year roommate in our introductory phone call, "but I have headphones. You won't have to hear them or anything."

"Okay," said Stephen from Maryland.

And that was that. We moved on to who would bring the TV, microwave, and mini-fridge. Thankful as I was for his indifference to what I had just told him, I tried not to react when he said his favorite music was Christian rock. What did I expect my roommate would listen to when the college's name announced its religious affiliation? How hard was it going to be to find friends with whom I had something in common?

At least my roommate seemed like a nice guy. I couldn't imagine a devout Christian gossiping about my eyes, as a few high school friends had done. "You know why J.T. grew a beard, don't you? Because he can't see his face to shave." This inaccuracy bothered me less than the fact that one more person had been informed of my vision problem.

Late August came faster than it ever had during high school. My parents and I joined the queue of freshmen waiting for their room keys. The line moved quickly. When I reached the front, the guy behind the table said nothing.

"Tell him your name," Mom whispered. I wasn't the only one who had made adjustments in the past year. My parents had become, like most good parents in their own ways, experts in the art of anticipation.

Not wanting to unpack anything until Stephen arrived, we made our way to the bookstore. As soon as we stepped through the door, one of the employees offered to help locate the books for my classes. Employees were helping all freshmen find their books, not only me. None of us knew where anything was, but this wouldn't last long, our shared oblivion.

"I have a voucher?" I told/asked the person behind the register.

"Hold on," the woman said, summoning the man working the other register. With all the discretion of an auctioneer, she said, "What do I do about a book voucher?"

My face flushed. I fixed my gaze on the counter, hoping none of my fellow students knew what a voucher was.

In the spring, I had begun meeting with a state agency called vocational rehabilitation. Because I met the blindness threshold, they would provide financial assistance with college, including books. Their help with room and board and a small amount of tuition, combined with my academic scholarship, made the cost of attending this pricey private school roughly what I would have paid at the state university. It felt wrong to receive money for not being able to do something. I wasn't being rehabilitated; I was going to college, just like two-thirds of the kids from my high school.

We returned to my room to find Stephen hammering a homemade loft he believed would maximize our limited space. He might have been right because less than three feet of clearance remained between his mattress and the ceiling.

Stephen's parents were significantly older than mine. They had gray hair and were, like their son, exceptionally polite. The six of us made our way to the dining hall for dinner, where the din of strangers in a room the size of a small supermarket stood my hairs on end.

Mom began describing for me, with practiced discretion, what choices I had at different stations. This was my only chance to memorize the location of foods. After today I was on my own. Mom started to ask one of the cafeteria workers if they printed weekly menus, but I cut her off. It felt as though people were staring at me, even if they weren't.

After dinner, Stephen and his parents drove to the Walmart twelve miles away. My parents left for their motel, letting me unpack so I'd know where to find everything. I was alone in my dorm room for the first time. The industrial-watt bulb in the ceiling, which Dad would install in all my fixtures at the start of each year, made it easier for me to see. It also made the stifling room even warmer. Only the senior dorms had air-conditioning.

Voices of people getting to know each other multiplied outside my open window. I had met my best friends, Rizwan and Joe, in eighth grade. We would talk regularly on the phone, see each other on holidays. Maybe I didn't need new friends.

My clothes fit easily in the chest of drawers and the open-faced closet. I alphabetized the twenty CDs I had selected less for how much I had been listening to them than for how many cool points they might earn me. I hardly ever listened to Pearl Jam anymore, but placed them face-out on the bookshelf Dad had made me. I hid the bulky four-track cassette player and all my textbooks on tape, *Recordings for the Blind and Dyslexic* stamped on every side, in a steamer trunk under my bed.

Laughter outside, male and female, sounded flirtatious. Already they're pairing off, I thought. An hour away in Morgantown, Rizwan was rooming with another of our high school friends. If I were there, they could vouch for me, introduce me to new people they'd met in class, assure everyone in our residence hall that I wasn't rude or aloof when I didn't return a nonverbal greeting.

Go outside, I told myself. What's stopping you? There's no danger in not recognizing anyone—nobody knows anybody. Yet. Sidle up to a cluster of people and introduce yourself. Where are you from? What's your major?

I lay down on the bed I had just made and closed my eyes. Was I going to cry? Don't cry. Your roommate's going to be back any minute. The musty pillow I had slept on for as long as I could remember reminded me I wasn't in my own room anymore. Homesick. That's what I was feeling. All of us, every single freshman, were leaving our homes, saying goodbye to our families, our childhood. A few tears were completely normal.

My orientation group was to meet under a large tree on the corner of campus. From there, we would walk to the house of the religion professor serving as our leader. Our group had met briefly the day before, students as well as parents, just long enough to say our names. In that short time, my parents had befriended half a dozen of their counterparts. Mom and Dad had been popular in high school. We bumped into someone they knew everywhere we went. Clearly the extrovert gene skips a generation.

When I didn't recognize the voices of the few students waiting by the tree, I feared this wasn't the right tree. I had only practiced the walk with my parents a single time before we said goodbye. Afterward, in the parking lot outside my dorm, Dad made a last-minute pitch for the college a few miles from our house. Mom asked one more time if I was going to be all right.

"I'll be fine," I said. If there was anything else to say, I didn't know how to say it.

Finally I placed the voice of a loud talker from yesterday's meeting. Someone said this get-together was a cookout, and my chest ballooned with anxiety. Nerve-racking as the cafeteria had been, would be, a cookout at a strange home, surrounded by strangers, was a gauntlet of horrors. Please don't make us assemble our own hamburgers. Please let the serving spoons in the baked beans or potato salad be made of dark plastic. Let the paper plates and plastic forks be easy to find. Let there be bottles or cans. No pitchers or two-liters.

I had a late lunch with my parents, I thought of saying. That would be my excuse if putting food on a plate presented any problems. It would be a long future of excuses, reasons, rationales—never lies.

I waited to be the last in line. This allowed me to go as slow as I wished. It also guaranteed only one set of eyes on me as I searched for enough food to constitute a meal. Thanks to the panic that came with eating around strangers, meals would become as utilitarian as showers and laundry. For most, the "freshman fifteen" refers to the weight gained from a steady diet of cafeteria food, but I would finally shed the fifteen pounds I had tried to lose since junior high.

Larger groups of people shrank to threes and fours as small talk grew into stories. Some, fearing they might be missing out on better topics or cooler people, flitted from group to group. A guy in a striped shirt who'd competed for the title of Mr. Teen Maryland regaled me with his weight-lifting exploits. If it didn't feel like the groundwork for a lasting friendship, the adjacent circle where the loud talker kept doing a Jim Carrey impersonation—Alrighty then! Alrighty then!—seemed at best a lateral move.

———

The next day our orientation group convened outside the library to obtain our student IDs. Together we would make our way upstairs and form a line, or so I assumed. Once we reached the second floor, the sight of velvet ropes foreshadowed a setup more complicated than a buffet.

"What's your last name?" the brunette in front of me asked the loud talker.

He told her it started with an *R*, and the brunette clapped her hands. She was an *S*.

It seemed unlikely that I would be in line with the *R*'s. I couldn't remember the last names of anyone else in my orientation group.

"Next," called a woman somewhere to my left.

I heard what might be a camera click. That they were taking our picture meant these IDs did not already exist. Would I have to write my name on a thin black line? Height? Weight? Major? Desire to donate organs?

The brunette and the loud talker disappeared into the carpeted void. The velvet rope ended to my left. The line behind me grew. I waited the interval of time the brunette had waited and made my way toward the tables, stopping at the first one I reached.

"Last name?"

I told her.

The woman behind the table let me know I needed another table. Less helpful was the manner in which she directed me to it: an arm pointed somewhere to the right.

I nodded. Maintaining eye contact, I said again, "Which table?"

Again she pointed, and I cast my gaze to the ceiling for a better look. I could see which direction she was pointing, but there were several tables in that direction, all of them with people on both sides. I nodded.

"Next," said the woman in the far corner where the camera clicked.

Somebody behind a table put a piece of paper in my hand. It was thick card stock. The girl in front of me leaned over the table to write on hers. I stepped backward out of line, if I had been in line. I made my way past the last table and kept going.

The metal bar in the center of a door against the back wall seemed consistent with an exit. I pushed it. There were stairs. Wonderful, plentiful stairs. I took them to the first floor. A door between sunny windows had to lead outside. When I pushed it, a bell slightly quieter than prisons used to signal a riot filled the stairwell.

I froze, realizing I had set off an alarm. I let the door close. After a few seconds, the alarm stopped.

On the second floor, the door leading to the stairwell opened. "It really does sound," chided an older woman who had made her way to the landing between floors.

"Sorry." I fabricated a self-deprecating smile. Silly me.

The librarian returned to the second floor.

I stared at the odd door that did and did not lead outside.

5
MAKE-BELIEVE

IN THE FIRST WEEKS of college, I ate most meals in my dorm room, listening to Geraldo Rivera interview pundits and peripheral figures in the O. J. Simpson murder trial. During parents' weekend, I tossed brick after brick of ramen into the grocery cart, and Dad asked if they still served food at the cafeteria.

When I ran out of groceries, I burned quickly through my flex dollars at the campus snack bar. With my parents' next visit weeks away, I finally accepted my roommate's offer to join him and his friends at the dining hall. Once there, I worried less about what I'd eat than the whereabouts of people in our group. I listened for their voices, trying to keep track of shirts so I could follow someone to our table.

One October evening the cafeteria was closed. Signs

directed us to a cookout on the lawn of the freshman girls' dorm. What was it with this school and cookouts?

I couldn't think of an excuse to return to my room. Whether or not Stephen's friends had become my friends, they were the only people I knew. Parting without a word might jeopardize my standing invitation to future meals.

"Sure you're not hungry?" This came from Melody, the incredibly sweet art major from Massachusetts. She wasn't asking me but Rebecca, the environmental science major who had balked at the lack of vegetarian options.

"I'll get an apple later," Rebecca said.

If either of them noticed I had not eaten, they didn't mention it. I had never gotten in line, saying I'd wait for the crowd to thin. Now Rebecca and I sat on the half-wall that encircled the girls' dorm, our other friends playing volleyball.

More often than not, Rebecca and I ended up beside or across from each other at dinner. Usually she was the only one who laughed at my jokes. Her own sense of humor veered toward the sardonic, and we were mutually chagrined by the Disney fare and PG-13 comedies our group gathered to watch on the campus's closed-circuit TV channel.

"So what do you think of Rebecca?" Stephen asked me on the walk back to our room from another movie night.

I knew what he was asking but didn't know how to answer.

What should be the easiest part of dating, knowing whether you're attracted to someone, wasn't a skill I had mastered since losing my sight. Standing directly in front of someone, my blind spots aimed at their face, I have a partial view of the body. The blind spots allow enough light and shadows for me to see most eyes, hair, an open mouth. *Notice* might be the more accurate verb. When wearing sunglasses, or when I'm sure someone isn't looking, I can cast my gaze skyward for a slightly better view, but faces are mysteries I'm rarely close enough to solve.

When people speak of love at first sight, they really mean attraction at first sight. Because sight for me becomes a factor much later in the equation, what I tend to experience is attraction at first everything else. So-and-so has a great personality, we sometimes say when so-and-so is not conventionally attractive, as though personality were not an extension of one's appearance. The voice, too, not only what we say but how it sounds, the timbre and volume, the confidence in our enunciation or lack thereof, our laugh and how often we share it—all of this lets people see us. It also reveals how we see ourselves and how we want to be seen. Not that we always know what to look for, or even what we see the first time we look.

I liked that Rebecca wrote poetry. In high school, one of her poems won a national contest open to writers of all ages. To a West Virginian for whom Mexican food meant Taco Bell, a vegetarian from Connecticut seemed exotic and worldly. In the seven years since my first and only relationship, a month-long, nonverbal affair of hand-holding on field trips, I had danced with a girl and gone with another to see a musical, neither of which, if success is measured in future dances and dates, could be called a success. On top of whatever had rendered me undatable through high school, I had become legally blind. What did I think of Rebecca? I felt lucky that someone so interesting might be interested in me.

I held my magnifier over Rebecca's picture in the freshman directory. It was too small to tell what she looked like, but even before Stephen confirmed that she liked me as more than a friend, before Rebecca accepted my invitation to the autumn dance, before two weeks of holding hands during movies with and without our friends around, before I finally brought my face close enough to see hers and kiss the first girl I had ever kissed, I didn't think I was attracted to her.

It was also through my roommate that I met an English major named Danny, though he wasn't among the people we sat with during meals.

"Whose poster is that?" Danny wanted to know. He came to return a book he had borrowed from Stephen.

"Which one?" I asked. All the posters in the room were mine, but I couldn't tell which wall he was looking at.

"*Rain Man.*"

I turned to my framed poster of the 1988 Oscar winner for Best Picture, Actor, Director, and Original Screenplay: an impervious-looking Tom Cruise in sport coat and sunglasses, Dustin Hoffman staring at the ground as they abscond from the institution. I told Danny it was mine.

"Great movie." Danny took a few steps into the room. "Are these yours, too?"

From a series of hollow clacks, I deduced he was checking out my movies rather than my CDs. I said they were.

"*Stand by Me,*" Danny said. "I need to see this again."

Heathers, *The Big Picture*, *A Few Good Men*. Each title became a rabbit hole of conversation. He thought Pacino in *Scent of a*

Woman was overacting, and I didn't disagree. I also didn't say I first watched it the summer I lost my sight, nor that what I loved about the movie, more flawed with each viewing—an entire day of the Thanksgiving weekend is unaccounted for—was how the blindness of Al Pacino's Lieutenant Colonel Frank Slade is subordinated by his brash charisma.

"He was an asshole before," says the nephew of the former Marine. "Now all he is is a blind asshole."

"Hoo-ah," replies Pacino.

I had recently moved my movie collection from under my bed to the bookshelf, an unanswered ad for friends with whom I had more in common than those I met through my roommate.

And moments later, Danny was gone. My cinephile soulmate was only here to return that book.

After Rebecca and I broke up the first week of our sophomore year, it was back to microwaved ramen in my dorm room. Stephen had taken a position as an RA, and I opted for a single over getting to know another stranger. Whenever I had an urge to experience campus life, I phoned Joe or Rizwan for stories of parties they had been to, girls they were seeing, gossip about high school classmates who had reinvented themselves in college as stoners, bisexuals, theater majors, Republicans.

From time to time, I managed to join acquaintances of Danny's in the cafeteria, positioning myself beside a free chair in hopes he would show up. The times he did, usually with his friend Ron, the future of my social life seemed on the line.

Whenever something I said made Danny laugh, the paused movie that my life had become started playing again. The rarer times Ron joined him in laughter, the movie changed from black and white to color.

Ron lived on the same floor of my residence hall, but we rarely spoke. Still dating his hometown girlfriend, he drove to her college most Fridays and didn't return until Sunday night. Along with Danny, he was one of the five students annually given a full ride, complete room and board, free textbooks, their own computer, and a magazine subscription of their choice. Unlike with Danny, my few attempts at conversation with Ron didn't go well.

"What's creative writing like?" I asked Ron upon learning he and Danny had taken the class as freshmen. I hadn't known it existed, let alone that you could major in creative writing.

"Basically," Ron said, hanging up dress shirts with a scholar's focus, "you make Xerox copies of your soul and everyone sits in a circle and says what's wrong with it."

I laughed. When he said nothing further, I slinked into the hallway and back to my room.

What I perceived as Ron's dislike of me I came to see as a healthy skepticism. Danny already had one reserved, sardonic sidekick of medium height and medium build. Did he need another? Neither Ron nor I was as good at making friends as holding on to them, as evidenced by his asking me, eight years later, to be the best man at his wedding. Three years after that, I would ask him to be mine.

To friends, my low vision wasn't a secret exactly. At the same time, I took great care to downplay the implications, to make people forget I was different. After my circle of high school friends contracted so thoroughly post-diagnosis, details about my blindness never felt like the best icebreaker.

"Wow, I never knew," friends sometimes said upon learning I was legally blind, and I'd swell with pride thinking of all I had managed to conceal. As for what acquaintances thought of me, the friends of friends, classmates, people I passed on sidewalks who didn't greet me by name, I took an out-of-sight, out-of-mind approach.

"I just thought you were an asshole," said a girl from my freshman orientation group, who became a good friend senior year. As a freshman, she had waved to me multiple times before giving up. She wouldn't be the last to confess this, and I was always relieved people thought I was an ass-hole and not blind.

Outdoors, sunglasses let me avoid accidental eye contact. For friends, this usually triggered a verbal greeting. Indoors, where only movie stars and blind people get to wear sun-glasses, I cultivated a look of focus: eyes straight ahead or off into the distance—the opposite distance from whichever direction someone might approach—mouth slightly ajar, brow furrowed as if in thought.

Danny and Ron seemed to notice more of what I couldn't see than my friends freshman year. One day, without prompting, Ron read me the menu outside the cafeteria. Danny knew to read me the new releases at the video store, but I never told either of them, while we watched movies, how little of them I could see. Another year would pass before I'd ask one of them for help finding the mall men's room. Until then, I'd hold it for the hour-long car ride back to campus.

My blindness was only one reason I felt like an impostor. The social caste system of high school was allegedly behind us, but I couldn't shake the feeling that these guys were out of my league. They listened to bands whose videos MTV only played at 3 a.m. I had only recently weaned myself off classic rock. Walking across campus, people shouted their names. Everyone passed me in silence.

Even their pain seemed superior to mine. The previous summer, Danny's girlfriend had died from a rare blood illness. The girl Ron thought he would marry recently left him for a Russian exchange student. All I had ever lost was my sight.

Hiding my blindness in class wasn't difficult. I only pretended to take notes, wadding pages filled with my illegible handwriting when I got to my room. For group work, the student doing the writing usually read the questions aloud. Knowing what the questions were didn't mean I could help with the answers, especially in labs. Nobody complained when I watched in silence, but they sometimes bristled when I asked for explanations, delaying our completion of the worksheet.

Early my freshman year, I had apologized to a professor for not contributing to the group assignment, reminding him I was the one with the bad eyes. I offered to complete an alternate activity, something I could do out of class. In high school, my teachers had gone to great trouble to give me anatomy exams by touch, make audio flash cards for Spanish, substitute weight lifting for soccer in phys ed.

The professor considered my offer, waving to students arriving for the next class. "I wouldn't worry about it," he said.

He meant it was a small assignment, one percent of our grade, and I'd receive the same credit as my group members who did all the work. What I heard was: It's less work for everyone if you keep that to yourself.

I started writing short stories my senior year of high school. One morning late in the fall, I peeked nervously around the cubicle of my English teacher, six double-spaced pages in my hand. If I gave her something I had written, would she read it and tell me what she thought?

"Is that it there?" Mrs. Jones, whom I'd had junior year as well, had the warm smile of a mother on a 1980s sitcom. She also had a way, throughout the year I was adjusting to vision loss, of knowing when I was asking for more than her time.

I handed her the first thing I had ever written that wasn't an assignment for school. My mom had typed it for me the night before. I hadn't yet learned how to type without seeing the screen or keyboard.

The plot centered on a conversation between a fellow of unspecified age and some kind of celestial gatekeeper. At the heart of their discussion was a riddle the man had to answer in order to get whatever one gets when riddles are posed by celestial gatekeepers. Did I mention the assassination of John F. Kennedy was involved? It was pretty deep, more philosophical than the pedestrian classics we had been reading for class.

"I don't think I get it," Mrs. Jones told me in her cubicle a week later. "Walk me through what's going on here."

"Which part?" The symbolism was pretty subtle. I was prepared to make it more accessible for a wider audience. Did English teachers have connections to people who published short stories?

Mrs. Jones stared at the first page. "All of it, really."

One winter afternoon sophomore year, I asked Danny if he would read the first chapter of my novel in progress. I had begun writing it the summer after freshman year. Danny wrote poems that were, as far as I was concerned, as good as anything in our textbook for contemporary poetry. It wasn't only his words but what he wrote about, what he had to say, that he had something to say. Recently he had penned an eight-page homage to *The Waste Land* about the death of his girlfriend, the title of which alluded to the chorus of the German version of David Bowie's "Heroes." Most of my poems were parodies of poems I had studied in school.

I opened the file on my computer and performed the keyboard shortcut for reducing the font to 12 points from my default setting of 240. This was the first time I had let someone other than my parents see my unadjusted font. Using my magnifier and a lot of spare time, I had taught myself how to spell-check using keyboard commands. Proofreading one word at a time was draining, but I preferred it to asking for help.

Throughout my freshman year, I needed an attendant in the computer lab to help me open a blank file. When I finished, I pressed CONTROL-P to print and carried my pages to the writing center. The writing center tutor, after marking my typos, returned with me to the computer lab to make corrections. The director of the writing center, suspecting her tutors were writing parts of my papers, arranged a meeting with the school's ADA compliance expert. Yes, he determined, a tutor was allowed to insert the *l* I had omitted from the word *clock*.

Danny sat in my desk chair and began to read. Mouse clicks signaled moves to a new page. I lay on my bed, listening to his occasional chuckles. The novel's main character was a writer sitting in the corner booth of a diner who, after thirty pages, had not moved from his booth or been joined in the narrative by other characters.

"Well?" I said when Danny got up from my desk.

He mentioned a couple of lines he had liked.

"It's still really rough," I said.

"Don't take this the wrong way," he said, "but I like your poetry better than your fiction."

The first thing I noticed about Cathryn was her hat. In the hall after creative writing, members of the English faculty debated what kind of hat it was. The flamboyant professor of British literature believed it was a derby.

"It's not a derby," said our creative writing professor, who seemed more like a droll Marine than the well-published poet I would learn he was.

Cathryn, blocking my path to the stairs, said she didn't know.

I couldn't really see the hat, but I said, "Maybe it's a bowler. There's sort of a *Clockwork Orange* thing going on."

Everyone laughed, three English professors and this quiet girl who was, judging from the attention she received from professors and other students, pretty attractive. I made a hasty, confident exit down the stairs, following the age-old advice of comedians and George Costanza to always leave them laughing.

Two days later, Cathryn was sitting beside me in creative writing. Without her hat, I didn't realize it was her until she said *hey*. Her friendly tone suggested we were people who hung out regularly. Because she never spoke in class beyond answering roll and periodically correcting the professor's pronunciation of her last name, it took me an extra beat to place her voice. "Hey" was all I could think to reply.

Leaving class, I asked if she had gotten to next week's story, by the guy who provided special instructions for it to be read slowly. In the first paragraph, he referred to semen as "precious communion." Each week I dropped off the handouts from my classes, including the work of other creative writing students, in the Learning Center for someone to record on cassette tapes. For three years, my reader was a cute psychology major uncannily named Patience. That she managed not to pause or audibly wince upon reading the aforementioned story might rank among the great feats of elocution.

Cathryn laughed. "Uh, yeah."

Danny knew Cathryn from Concert Chorale, one of his four dozen extracurricular activities. It was outside his room where I next bumped into her, the evening before most of us were leaving for Thanksgiving break. Cathryn had a coat on, keys jangling in her hand.

"You should bring it back with you," she said when I mentioned a Janis Joplin boxed set at my parents' house.

"I'll try to remember," I said, and slid it into my backpack the first hour I was home.

The following Sunday we sat in my room, serenaded by the caterwauling of Port Arthur, Texas's favorite daughter. I related anecdotes from two Joplin biographies I had read in high school. Despite the adoration of fans and fellow musicians, Janis never ceased to see herself as the outcast high school classmates called ugly. A deep loneliness lasted until her death at age twenty-seven, like the Texas accent she never managed to shake.

For the first time, I noticed Cathryn's West Virginia accent. As diligently as I had polished away my own regional inflections, I kind of liked it on her. It came and went, and when it came she seemed to wield it as a tool of flirtation, a vocal batting of eyelashes.

Cathryn told me how much she loved her younger brother, that her father worked the swing shift at some kind of factory, that her mother had left them when she was little. The latter she relayed with a matter-of-factness that didn't invite follow-up questions. It was the same tone in which I told her about my optic nerves walking out when I was sixteen.

At some point, we moved from the rug on my floor to my bed, me and this English major with the long brown hair. I thought I was attracted to her, as much as I could be without bringing my face inches from hers. We had been talking since ten o'clock. The sound of showers on the other side of my door meant it was now around seven. Doing the math, it seemed a decent bet that if I kissed her she might kiss me back. She did.

Cathryn's eyes were closed while we kissed. I left mine open, relieved to feel what I hadn't felt with Rebecca. After a minute, I let my eyes close, not because I wanted to but because I could.

What I missed most after losing my sight, more than individual tasks like driving or reading, was the sense of possibility, of choices. For better or worse, there are substitutes for getting places. There are alternatives to printed text. It was the times I had to make a selection—when presented with a menu, while shopping for CDs or groceries, while standing at a wall of colorful rectangles in a video store—when I most felt the world had shrunk beyond recognition.

Because Danny and I rented movies so voraciously, most of our trips weren't quick grabs from the new releases. We moved from wall to wall in an archaeological dig for some 1970s classic one of us vaguely remembered Siskel or Ebert referencing five years ago. With the Internet still learning to crawl, our memories and Danny's eyes were our only search engines. The utter disregard of Buckhannon's video stores for genre and the Roman alphabet lengthened our searches, but we had nowhere else to be on a Saturday afternoon.

Danny read me the back of the sleeves, sometimes in an accent, sometimes in an impersonation of one of our professors. I felt guilty when we couldn't rent a movie with subtitles. I had been getting into foreign films—*Le Grand Chemin* and

Tie Me Up! Tie Me Down!—when my eyes insisted on more provincial fare.

Unable to help Danny look, I did my best to provide hot takes of critics I remembered from my years loitering in the cinema aisle of Waldenbooks and B. Dalton. No longer able to skim books or magazines, I acquired as much information as I could from TV, radio, conversations within earshot. I became a news junkie, hoarding information in an attempt to compensate for my low vision, hoping my stores of trivia made me better company in situations where I could feel like a burden. When I had no information to offer, I tried to earn my keep with witty comments.

On college student budgets, meals out usually meant Burger King or the Elkins Taco Bell, restaurants whose menus I knew as well as the chronology of Oscar winners from the last thirty years. The rare times a menu did appear before me—at Audrey's all-night diner, where the specials fluctuated depending on the frozen offerings at the nearby Sam's Club—Danny or Ron began reading me what they had before I could ask them to.

Cathryn and I had been dating for a few months before we ever went on a date. She chose one of the chain restaurants near the Clarksburg mall that sold their appetizers in the grocer's freezer. My menu lay sideways when I picked it up, and I figured the side without photos was the front, hoped I wasn't about to stare at an upside-down menu.

I could always order whatever Cathryn ordered, but by now we were in a relationship, not merely *hanging out*. In a few years, I'd learn the trick of asking servers for specials or recommendations. Today I stared at the swirling colors in front of me, my heart beating as it hadn't since our first kiss.

My not being able to read a menu wasn't news. Most days she joined me for lunch and dinner with Danny and Ron, and we always paused inside the entrance for someone to read the day's entrées.

"Could you, um . . ." I looked at her over my opened, probably-not-but-I-still-wasn't-absolutely-sure-it-wasn't-upside-down menu.

"What?"

"I'm not entirely sure what they have," I said.

Cathryn looked at me for a moment before it sank in. "Oh. Do you want me to read the whole thing?"

"Just start with the headings."

She read me the categories. When she reached the sandwiches and burgers, I had her list individual items. Given the faint tone of what I thought was disappointment, I only asked for a couple of descriptions.

The college's other creative writing professor was the state's poet laureate. Hers was the only faculty bio that listed books and awards. She had grown up on a nearby farm and had only returned to West Virginia, somebody said, to care for an ailing father.

With only six students in the class, the poet laureate decided our fiction workshop would meet in her office rather than a classroom. She was friendly and warm, calling us by our names by the end of the first day. Her syrupy accent belied the obvious genius of everything she told us.

We had heard that one of the poet laureate's former students, a novelist who had grown up in this tiny town, had been nominated for the National Book Award. This writer's short stories regularly appeared in *Rolling Stone*, *Esquire*, and *Playboy*. Two of the poet laureate's recent protégées, friends of Danny's, currently attended graduate programs in creative writing.

Learning that there was such a thing as a master of fine arts, that a creative writing major might lead to a stable job, even if the only job seemed to be teaching creative writing, led me to declare an English major. I had originally declared psychology as a freshman, but had no passion for it. It had only seemed, as physical therapy had seemed before that, like something someone with low vision could do.

I could teach, I thought. Writing on a chalkboard wouldn't present any problems, given how big teachers had to write for people in the back to read it, not that my English professors did much writing on the chalkboard. I wouldn't see students raise their hands, but most people in my English classes didn't wait to be called on. In classes as small as my fiction workshop, I could even feign eye contact.

For three hours on Wednesday evenings, six of us crowded into four chairs, the floor, and windowsill of the poet laureate's office. The other students were Danny, Cathryn, two guys who identified as poets, and, awkwardly enough, my freshman-year girlfriend, Rebecca.

The poet laureate began each class by reading us a passage from something she had recently enjoyed, and we all tried to say smart things about the piece this woman we all hoped would be our mentor thought brilliant enough to share. Two months into the semester, the passage she read to us sounded familiar.

"Do you know who wrote that?" she asked us, smiling.

Nobody did. Nobody except for me. She had read us the short essay I had handed in the week before.

College had finally become college. By the summer before my junior year, I had reinvented myself as a guy who wrote short stories, who had a girlfriend, who had sex. That I spent my summers in a different house from the one where I grew up, my parents having moved to a split-level contemporary in the Charleston suburb of Kanawha City, seemed to underscore how far I had come since high school.

For the first time since second grade, we had city water, a paved driveway, central air, a street address rather than a route number. The location was convenient to sidewalks and bus routes, not that I ever used them. From my upstairs bedroom atop a steep driveway that petrified everyone who ascended it, I could glimpse flickers of traffic on MacCorkle Avenue, cars en route to wherever it was people in cars went all day.

Most summer days I awoke around noon and consumed a steady diet of *Golden Girls* and *Beverly Hills, 90210* reruns. The thought of leaving the house by myself never occurred to me. Compared to a ten-by-twelve dorm room, our new house felt like living in a mall. As Chief Brody says in *Jaws*, when asked why someone afraid of the water would live on an island, "It's only an island if you look at it from the water."

The road running in front of our driveway had no sidewalk. Say I managed to hug mailboxes and driveways for the hundred-foot trek to the 50th Street railroad tracks, the other side of which led to the sidewalk-lined MacCorkle Avenue, where would I have gone? Foodland? Tudor's Biscuit World? Let's say I took the back streets with their pedestrian-friendlier stop signs, avoiding all traffic lights and the unpredictable cars that terrified me no less than great white sharks, and made it to the mall on 57th Street. This wasn't the Charleston Town Center, mind you, but the Kanawha Mall, an island of misfit stores that ceded half its parking lot each summer to a traveling carnival.

"Good evening. I'm Tom Brokaw, and this is the *NBC Nightly News*. We begin tonight with the story of nineteen-year-old English major James Tate Hill, who was struck and killed this afternoon while walking to the Kanawha Mall, the inferior of Charleston, West Virginia's two malls. Found in his pocket was a 22× loupe magnifier, which Hill might have used to identify Elton John's *Greatest Hits Volume II*, but only if no one was around to judge his inability to read the print on a compact disc. The fictional characters from *The Golden Girls* and *Beverly Hills, 90210* could not be reached for comment."

During the school year, I was in constant motion: to class, upstairs, downstairs, the cafeteria, girlfriends' dorms, the Learning Center, the campus snack bar. I walked everywhere I needed to be. Conveniently, the only places I needed to be were buildings on our small campus. With friends, I had navigated the sidewalks that led to town. I could have walked them by myself if I wanted to, I liked to think, but never wanting to was much easier.

As much as I missed Cathryn, as much as I missed Danny and Ron, as much as I missed college and its illusion of independence, none of it felt real. I had known my girlfriend fewer than six months, my new friends less than a year. It's hard to trust relationships so young. It's hard to trust that people like you when so much of yourself remains hidden.

Over the summer, I didn't have to pretend I could see anything. I read books on tape and watched TV with my bedroom door closed. If I was feeling sociable, I left the door open, but my parents and I had fallen into a don't-ask, don't-tell policy with regard to my blindness. The same was true of Rizwan, still my best friend, who picked me up a few times a week to wander the Town Center or drive around Charleston with the windows down, Nas or Notorious B.I.G. rattling the back windshield.

My friendship with Riz began in eighth grade when I whispered across our homeroom, did he want to be locker partners? In my bolder days, which coincided with an ability to catch someone's eye across a room, I had fewer qualms about making the first move.

Our paths hadn't crossed in seventh grade, though Riz's name came up frequently in conversations with mutual friends. Though born in America, he was the son of Pakistani immigrants, his father a civil engineer and his mother a department store manager. Like so many Asian and South Asian kids in our mostly white junior high, he was the target of bullying by the remedial, mulleted students in frayed army jackets. Unlike most of their victims, who tried to ignore their racial slurs, Riz fought back. He had a method of luring them within earshot of teachers, getting them in trouble without being punished for his own profanity.

Our senior year of high school, Riz's father died. He had battled cancer for some time, though his death came suddenly. I waited a week after the funeral before calling.

"How are you doing?" I asked, the only time I would ever inquire about his loss.

"I'm all right," he said. "Let me call you back," he added. Lots of family were still in town.

We never revisited the subject. Maybe he was following my lead after the loss of my vision months earlier. Maybe, like me, he was a teenage boy who didn't have words to describe his emotions. With a twelve-year-old sister, a six-year-old brother, and a grieving mother to take care of, he didn't have time to worry how he felt.

Months later, Riz invited me to Myrtle Beach with his family. We walked for hours down the shore, back to our hotel along the sidewalk, ducking into air-conditioned stores to cool off. Inside a magic shop, a teenager behind the register asked if we wanted to see some card tricks. We watched him deal cards on a pale counter.

"Are you blind?" the kid asked me after his first trick.

My heart pounded. Quickly I tried to establish eye contact with my accuser. "No, why?"

"You weren't looking at the cards," he said.

I pushed out a laugh. "I guess we partied a little too hard last night."

Riz joined me in laughter, letting this amateur magician know the mistake was his, not mine.

The following summer, days before we'd leave for another beach trip, I accompanied Riz to the car dealership to pick up the family's new 4Runner. It was the first new car they had owned since he was in elementary school. From there, we drove to the cemetery where his father was buried, his little sister and baby brother in the backseat.

"We'll be right back," Riz told me, parking outside the gate. He hadn't explained what they were here to do, but it was obvious. Close friends tell each other everything. Best friends never have to.

Cathryn sent me letters throughout the summer, using a font large enough for me to read them with my 15× magnifier: updates on what she had been doing, what she missed about me, when she might be able to drive to Charleston for a visit. My letters back to her stretched mall outings with Riz into picaresque adventures spanning seven single-spaced pages.

We talked on the phone twice a week. We sent each other mixtapes with recorded messages between songs, but it was the letters, with their black, irrevocable ink, the pages so thick they sometimes split the seams of envelopes, that reassured me we would make it.

Junior year I abandoned my single for an on-campus apartment with Danny, Ron, and our sophomore-year RA, Mark. It had a small kitchen, but I stayed on the meal plan because Cathryn wouldn't have anyone to eat with. We soon discovered that without Danny and Ron across the table from us, without the need to say how much we missed each other, conversation didn't come easily.

Cathryn and I became DJs at the campus radio station, a

37-watt outfit reaching, on the clearest night, the outskirts of our tiny town. DJs chose handles in lieu of real names. I was Jack London, and Cathryn, Virginia Woolf. That we didn't say much between songs didn't feel like a problem. That the times Danny filled in for her felt like fun rather than a two-hour commitment didn't seem like a big deal. You were supposed to have fun with your friends. Your girlfriends were for loving you, and vice versa.

Some days I told Cathryn I was just going to eat something in the apartment or grab a burger from the drive-through with Danny. Every one of these times, when I asked what she had eaten, the answer was "some chips" or "I don't remember. Just some crackers, I think."

"Why didn't you go to the cafeteria?"

"Because I didn't want to," she said, offended by the question.

When I opted to go off the meal plan, I wasn't sure if it had more to do with Cathryn's food choices than with the desire to have other people around while we ate. Still nineteen, the thought of cooking appealed to me as much as cleaning the bathroom, which, incidentally, I can't recall my roommates or me doing one time in the eight and a half months we occupied that apartment.

Shopping for groceries was a lot like shopping for CDs. I needed help finding anything smaller than cereal boxes, bags of Doritos, two-liters of Diet Coke. Compounding the struggle was my having no idea what I was supposed to be buying.

"What are you looking for?" Cathryn asked.

I pretended to eye the produce. A year into our relationship, I had managed to avoid so many of these situations, enough that she seemed to think a ride to the store was all I needed to shop for groceries. Were my performances truly that convincing, or had Cathryn convinced herself I was capable of so much more than I was?

"Salad," I said. It was the only meal I could think of that one could make from produce.

"Okay," she said. "What do you want in it?"

"You decide," I said, putting her in charge of the search.

A few aisles later, I asked Cathryn for meal ideas, deciding there was no shame in a nineteen-year-old guy not knowing what to cook. My shame lay in not seeing what occupied the shelves, shame I tried to allay by grabbing something—a bag of chips, a box of cornflakes, cans of Campbell's soup—whenever familiar logos came into focus, even if I had no particular desire for these products. Look at me, finding exactly what I'm looking for.

By our second trip to Kroger, Cathryn's bemused assistance had soured into frustration. Verbal responses became wordless reaches for freezer doors. Weeks later, she was throwing boxes in the cart so hard they came home with dents.

For every can and jar and bag whose shelf coordinates I memorized so I could locate them without help, there were new items we were trying to find for the first time because one of us had grown tired of our limited menu. Despite having cooked for herself and her younger brother as a teenager while their father worked the swing shift, Cathryn's cooking acumen surpassed mine only in her willingness to touch raw meat for Hamburger Helper.

My own frustration with her lack of contributions—these weren't elaborate meals, but I was doing most of the boiling and microwaving, and one hundred percent of the purchasing—bubbled over each time a frozen pizza smacked the cage of our shopping cart.

I didn't remember my eyes being a problem when I was with Rebecca. Because neither of us had a car, it had been easier to forget I couldn't drive. Except for walks to Dairy Queen and the city park, Rebecca and I rarely left campus. The few times we found ourselves in a restaurant whose menus didn't hang above the heads of cashiers, Rebecca read them to me in a hushed voice, the smart girl helping the slacker cheat on his test. One time at the two-screen movie theater in the neighboring town, we arrived during the previews, the lights already dimmed. The friends we had come with hurried to find seats before my eyes could adjust to the darkness, and Rebecca knew to reach for my hand.

Like Cathryn, Rebecca never asked about my eyes. I had given her all relevant information in the same stoic manner in which I debriefed professors and new acquaintances, the same way I had told Cathryn. It's no big deal, I tried to convey. What I was doing, a future girlfriend would point out to me, was shutting down the subject before it could be explored. But so often Rebecca intuited the help I needed before I asked, and I was so grateful not to have to ask. Not speaking of it, not reminding others of it, not letting it hang like a banner above my head let me almost forget, and to almost forget was to make it almost untrue.

Our grocery store stalemates metastasized to the rest of

the time we spent together. An argument over which two items we should get on a Domino's pizza provoked a tearful, hours-long conversation about our long-term compatibility. An offhand comment Danny made about labor unions, which I did not condemn, led to Cathryn not speaking to Danny or me for three days.

Our arguments seemed to worsen when Cathryn ordered me brochures for a graduate writing program at a university in Ohio. She was considering the school's journalism program. I had never heard of the writers on the faculty, which doubtless said more about me than the faculty. I wasn't ready, in the middle of my junior year, to start thinking about grad school.

"When will you be ready?" said Cathryn, and I realized we were talking about more than graduate school.

I should have asked why she wanted to be together after college when being together now seemed to frustrate her so much. If I'd had more experience in relationships, I might have known what to say, what to ask. Instead, I offered my usual response to questions I couldn't answer: a long silence.

Because Cathryn said hi to a lot of people, I had the impression when we met that she had a large network of friends. Once we were dating, it seemed she wasn't close enough to any of them to actually hang out. Her best friend—her only friend, as far as I could tell, beyond Danny and Ron—was a girl from high school with whom she hadn't spoken in nearly a year. Perhaps to a girl who had not seen her mother since third grade, whose father and brother never visited her at college, who returned for holidays to the now-empty house where she grew up, her father having moved in with a girlfriend, I was better than nothing.

When an internship kept Cathryn in her hometown for most of our school's January term, trips to the grocery store in Danny's newly acquired Civic became the kind of stress-free trips they had been with my grandmother as a child. With his infinite patience, I dared inquire about the nutritional content of all my processed foods. Thin as I had been since starting college, I wasn't sure if my chubbier teenage body was gone for good or merely in remission. I wondered the same about the tension between Cathryn and me. Her absence dimmed the memory of our fall bickering, but I didn't miss her as I had over the summer. When we ventured to Kroger again in early February, falling into our familiar silence, the contrast to the peaceable trips to the supermarket with Danny was overwhelming.

After putting away groceries, we ended up in the bedroom I shared with Danny. No one else was in the apartment. I lay down on the bed without taking my coat off. Sophomore year it was always snowing, but this was the year the temperature rarely rose above single digits.

"What's wrong?" Cathryn sounded annoyed.

I fixed my gaze on my desk, refusing to look at her. The truth was I could see her better when I wasn't looking at her. If she knew this, she never seemed to understand. I certainly never clarified.

"What's wrong?" she repeated, annoyance giving way to concern.

It took me a long time to speak. My voice quavered, seemed to fall into itself. "Why do you get like that?"

"Like what?"

I shook my head.

Cathryn sat beside me on my bed, on the blue comforter about which she had written a poem last year. If she responded, I didn't hear her over my sobs. I buried my face in the pillow. She lay beside me, her face pressed to my back. Now she was crying.

"I can't do things," I tried to say. I must have gotten it out because Cathryn, in a tear-cracked voice of her own, said, "I know."

I couldn't remember the last time I had cried. I had shed tears over the loss of my sight, but never like this. After three and a half years, a dam had finally cracked, splintered into pieces.

But everything was going to get better, I believed. This crying jag was my line in the sand: no more arguments, no more silent dinners, no more passive-aggressive standoffs at the grocery store. Instead, everything got worse.

The coming weeks saw, in no particular order: Cathryn refusing to join my roommates and me for dinner on my birthday; me throwing away the graduate school brochures she had given me; Cathryn getting drunk and me sulking about it because I didn't drink; Cathryn possibly breaking up with me by throwing the amethyst ring I had given her for Christmas onto my bed; me listening to David Bowie's "Life on Mars" on repeat for several hours; Cathryn flirting with our friend R.J., who was gay; me talking until sunrise with one of the girls who lived next door to our apartment, parting with a hug that Ron, who was going through his own breakup and taking personal offense at Cathryn's hostility toward me, casually mentioned the next time he saw Cathryn, resulting in the toss onto my bed of the amethyst necklace I had given her our first Valentine's Day. None of this felt as important, as decisive, as the argument in which I sarcastically apologized for not being able to drive Cathryn around like some archetypal boyfriend out of the 1950s.

"Maybe I like being driven around," she said—with enough composure that I could tell it wasn't solely an attempt to hurt me.

I'd like to report this was when I walked away, my dignity intact. Reader, it was not. Like the little boy at the beginning of *Big*, told he isn't tall enough to ride the rides the pretty girl is in line to ride, the rejection only made me want her more. But there was no Zoltar machine granting wishes for the restoration of enough sight to drive a car.

I couldn't help thinking I deserved this, that it was karma for how callously I had broken up with Rebecca two years earlier. As a reward for making the dean's list, my parents had bought me a plane ticket to visit her in Connecticut over the summer. For six days and five nights, I had never been more homesick. Everything felt wrong, from the tight quarters of her parents' townhouse to how much older her parents were than mine, from her mother's sodium-free cooking to how short Rebecca had cut her hair. Her once-edgy taste in music was veering uncomfortably toward mainstream radio; in recent weeks, she had purchased CDs by Hootie & the Blowfish and Blues Traveler. Even the beach we visited felt like a poor facsimile of all the beaches I had been to: shards of broken seashell where sand should be, the whoosh of traffic over our shoulders, not a soul venturing into the water. We spent a lot of time in used CD stores, Rebecca tirelessly reading me the track listings of album after album.

In cultures with arranged marriage, attraction is beside the point. Compatibility is beside the point. The couple meet and over time, as they forge a life together, love comes into view like a developing photograph. But our picture had already come into focus. And the problem, I kept reminding myself, wasn't what I could see. Long before our faces drew close enough that we closed our eyes and let our lips take over, I hadn't felt what I hoped to feel. After breaking up with her, I was terrified this would happen to me again, that I might never fall in love with someone who made my pulse flutter when I looked at her, and I promised myself that if I did, and she loved me back, I would hold on tight and not let go.

"I'm eighteen years old. I don't even know what love is." This was all I could think to tell the girl who had been nothing but kind to me for nearly a year.

Rebecca agreed, not yet aware of what I was telling her.

I felt shallow and ungrateful. I was also exhausted, pretending to feel something I didn't feel. I already spent so much energy living my other lie.

"I love you," said Rebecca, still unclear we were breaking up.

"I love you, too," I said, and it was as true as it was a lie.

Without enough students to fill an advanced fiction writing class, the course became an independent study with the poet laureate. Every few weeks we met to discuss a new short story I had written. At one point, I asked if she thought I could maybe think about graduate school in creative writing.

"Absolutely," she said.

Stunned by her response, I asked which programs were good ones, and she searched her bookshelves for a directory of writing programs. Weeks later, I named some schools and asked if I had a chance of getting in.

"Why wouldn't you?" she said.

My final project for the independent study was a portfolio of three revised stories from the semester. Because she was going on sabbatical next year, her comments on these stories would be the last feedback I received from her.

My self-addressed, stamped envelope arrived in early June. Carrying it to my room, I flipped to the last page of each story, where she usually wrote most of her comments. Sometimes it took me an hour to decipher cursive, if I could read it at all, but few things made me shiver like a check mark in the margins from the poet laureate.

I held my magnifier against the paper and examined all the white spaces. I checked the sides of every page. I smoothed the creases and scanned the backs of all three stories. I brought the pages to my dad in the living room. He confirmed the poet laureate hadn't made a single mark.

———

Persevere. This was the simple answer of an award-winning novelist when asked if he had any advice for young writers. The biggest difference between writers who make it and writers who don't is the ability to weather rejection, not giving up, lasting. As I entered my senior year of college, the words of wisdom I took to heart came not from this author but from the film *Animal House*. "My advice to you," Bluto tells Flounder, thrusting a six-pack into his hands, "is to start drinking heavily."

For the first three years of college, when friends asked why I didn't drink, I cited the uncertain effects on my eyes. It wasn't a lie exactly. Having never drunk so much as a wine cooler, I was technically uncertain what the effects would be, though my doctors seemed confident I could drink in moderation without harming my already-damaged optic nerves. The real reason I lasted so long without getting drunk, besides hating the taste of every alcoholic beverage I ever tried, was how stupid drunk people always seemed. Why were they so goddamn happy?

What they never told us in all those *Afterschool Specials* about booze, hooch, rotgut, the hard stuff, is how good it makes you feel. And since the perils of drink have been articulated ad nauseam, let us take this opportunity to praise the talents of John Barleycorn. For one, he does a bang-up job of letting you forget what you'd rather not remember: how uncomfortable you are around people you don't know or even particularly like, how silly the entire enterprise of dancing is, how many girls have seemed indifferent to you over the years—in stark contrast to these girls who suddenly seem so riveted to your every hilarious word now that you have a drink in your hand. Maybe they, too, are simply forgetting how average you are.

After half a dozen Sea Breezes or apricot brandy shots— I never was the manliest of drinkers—I added big-ticket items to my wish list of the briefly forgotten, namely being legally blind and not knowing what I'd be doing next year. Anxieties about what I couldn't see disappeared into the vortex of my blind spots. If I missed a step, couldn't find the men's room in a club, didn't see someone waving to me across a crowded room—or a not-so-crowded room—well, I must be pretty wasted, I readily offered, whether I was or not.

During my year of magical drinking, I managed to avoid falling in love, sometimes by choice and sometimes not. Hearing that Cathryn, within weeks of our breakup, had converted to Mormonism and gotten engaged to someone in her home-town made it tempting to think our problems had been her problems. Instead, every time I kissed a girl, my mind raced toward the inevitable moment when physical compatibility wouldn't be enough.

It would take a special person to date J.T., said a girl Danny dated for a tumultuous couple of months our senior year. Danny relayed her statement to me as evidence of what a cruel, fucked-up human being she was. What a bitch, I agreed, keeping it to myself how right she was.

One by one, envelopes arrived from the MFA programs to which I had applied. The school in North Carolina wished me luck in finding the program that was the right fit. The university in Virginia, where Danny had been offered admission in poetry, let me down with a reminder of how subjective writing is.

The problem with wanting to be an artist is that wanting to be one doesn't mean you get to be one. If you earn your degree in psychology, go to graduate school, and pass the requisite tests, you usually get to be a psychologist.

Throughout my senior year of high school, I continued to write stories and show them to Mrs. Jones. One story, about a lonely man wrongly accused of killing his wife in a fire, Mrs. Jones seemed to like far more than anything else I had written. She told me what to revise and, when I showed her a new draft, asked if she could teach it to our class.

"Do what?" I said.

"We'll use a pen name, of course."

But wouldn't it be obvious this story wasn't written by some long-dead master? Who wouldn't realize these photocopied, double-spaced, word-processed pages written by someone named J. Griffith Chaney—my pseudonym was the birth name of Jack London—were a literary sham of the highest order? That particular worry was put to rest the day Mrs. Jones distributed copies of my story. One of my classmates, the guy who gave all our teachers nicknames only he ever used, came into the library complaining about "Jonesy" giving us more work a week and a half before graduation.

"She must love this story," he said. "Look: she typed the freaking thing herself."

The day after we discussed "Bane" in class, Mrs. Jones gave me a stack of papers on which she had everyone write what they thought of it. One of the smartest students called it "the worst thing we've read in this entire class."

A year later, at Rebecca's urging, I entered "Bane" in a contest in her hometown sponsored by a national brand of pens. The evening I broke up with her, she had come to my room to deliver the book in which they published my winning story. Its cover was beige cardstock. The pages were 8.5-by-11-inch printer paper folded widthwise and bound by a pair of staples. That a story written by a sixteen-year-old had placed first in the fiction category open to writers of all ages from anywhere in the United States couldn't have said much about the competition. By then, at the wizened age of eighteen and a half, I could see my story's myriad flaws. Clearly Mrs. Jones wanted to teach it because I had lost my sight, not because I was the next Jack London.

One graduate school had not yet made their decision: the granddaddy of creative writing programs, the famed Iowa Writers' Workshop. The poet laureate had taught there as a visiting writer a few years ago. Her former student, the National Book Award nominee, had gone there, and my fingers were crossed that a letter of recommendation from the poet laureate would carry some weight.

The thin envelope arrived in early April. As many times as I had held my magnifier against the brochure, I thought I recognized the Iowa logo with my naked eye. I ducked into the men's room across from the post office, locked the stall, and got my 22× loupe out of my backpack.

"Our admissions process is highly competitive," said the graduate school. The letter-by-letter pace of my reading allowed my mind to jump to a dozen conclusions before the end of each sentence. Thin envelopes are the ones to fear, went the conventional wisdom, but this hadn't been the case when applying to college.

"This year we received eight hundred seventy-two applications in fiction for only twenty slots. Unfortunately . . ." continued the letter that completed my set of rejections.

Graduation morning Danny helped me find my spot in line behind a women's basketball player a head and a half taller than me. The air of late May was humid with hints of summer, but my hands were freezing. By contrast, my cheeks and forehead were on fire. High school graduation had been prefaced by a rehearsal lasting an entire afternoon, giant X's and arrows of bright-colored tape pointing us where to walk, stand, and exit the stage once we had our diplomas. Worried about the lack of a rehearsal for college graduation, I had gotten up extra early to do a practice walk-through.

As soon as I stepped through the doors of Rockefeller Gym, an older woman in a churchy ensemble blocked my path. I explained my intentions.

"You want to do what now?"

I repeated my request. "My eyes are bad," I clarified.

Betty White's evil twin said I shouldn't worry about anything.

"I just—I'm not sure if I can see where I—"

"You're graduating today," she said in a tone both saccharine and stern. "Just be a graduate."

Maybe if I had led with the eyesight, made a bigger deal of

it, called someone earlier in the week to make arrangements, I would have been granted access. I had grown a little complacent about the surroundings I came to know so well, arriving to unfamiliar classrooms only a few minutes prior to the first class rather than days before the semester began. Now here I stood in my cap and gown, stomach dipping as the first notes of "Pomp and Circumstance" played in the distance.

One by one they called our names, bodies in front of me disappearing like jumpers from a plane. Names echoed in the high ceiling, the staticky din of applause that had not subsided since the first graduate was announced. Then the women's basketball player, my last line of defense, was gone. The syllables in the air sounded a lot like my own name.

An older man in a cap and gown—the dean? the president?—handed me a leather rectangle. Another man on my right, also in cap and gown, shook my hand. To my left, a gap between him and a third man widened to reveal the chairs on the floor where we'd sat upon first entering the gym, where I understood I was to return now that I had my diploma. I took a step toward the opening.

Later that night and for countless nights in the coming weeks, months, years, this scene would play on a loop in my mind. I take one more step sideways, toward the white and black gowns of graduates already seated. Somewhere among the thousands of onlookers in the bleachers, my parents look on, one of them filming with the camcorder so my ill grandmother can watch the family's first college graduate receive his degree. I don't see any steps, so it must not be far from stage to floor. When I lower my leg to the hardwood, it finds only air, and I tumble sideways, the four-foot drop intermi-nable, my fall broken only by my leather-encased diploma. The wind is knocked out of me. Someone in the front row helps me to my feet, asks if I am okay. Names continue to echo through the rafters, but no one crosses the stage, the gaze of two thousand students and their families, professors, and the commencement speaker, the governor of West Virginia, fixed on the fallen graduate woozily bracing himself on the edge of the stage.

But this was not my fate. I did step sideways toward the edge of the stage. I looked beyond it into the abyss, saw the black and white gowns of graduates already seated. Uncer-tain where to go, where I was, I froze. One of the older men wrapped a hand around my arm. The other man did the same, one of them encouraging me forward with two giant pats on my back.

"Go forward?" I said, my voice barely audible over cheer-ing families.

The man who had handed me my diploma nodded hugely, his placating smile inches from my face.

I took a step forward and paused. Another step. I waited half a beat for someone to stop me and, when they didn't, kept going. At the end of the stage, I noticed the rug beneath my feet leading to the aisle through which we had entered the gym. I turned into the first row, whose outer folding chair was not occupied, and took my seat beside the women's bas-ketball player.

My time onstage felt like minutes, but camera footage would show that the president and dean's negotiations with

an obviously petrified graduate lasted nine seconds. That evening, trying to downplay how bad it looked, Mom told me
several other students had paused onstage to pose for photo-
graphs, but I doubted anyone in attendance mistook my timid
movements for saying cheese. When we took the video to my
grandparents' house the next day, carefully edited footage
would show me accepting my diploma and an abrupt cut to
my exit from the stage. Let Mawmaw believe, for the last few
months of her life, that her grandson was an ordinary college
graduate, indistinguishable from four hundred others in the
sea of caps and gowns.

6

INCREDIBLE
SHRINKING
WORLD

HALF AN HOUR FROM the Pennsylvania border, Morgan-town, West Virginia, is a city of thirty thousand largely made up of the university you nearly attended as an undergraduate. You've been accepted into the master's program in English. It isn't creative writing, but neither is it moving back home with your parents.

Your monthly budget is $476, the Social Security check you've received since turning eighteen. As part of the mental gymnastics required to convince yourself you are neither disabled nor blind, you regard the check as something between an inheritance and laundered money. The only apartments these checks can afford are efficiencies with hot plates and buzzing fluorescent lights reminiscent of bug zappers. Reluctantly you accept your parents' offer to help with rent and sign the lease for a one-bedroom in a building that used to be, someone tells you in a few months, a psychiatric hospital.

Arriving early for your first class, you find an empty class-room whose lights are off. A few days ago, in your practice walk to all your classes, a janitor confirmed you were in the right building. You feel the minute hand of your tactile watch. Twentieth-century American Literature should begin in one minute and you remain the only person in the room. A short walk takes you to Stansbury Hall, home of the English depart-ment. The rooms with open doors seem like offices, and none of the sounds resemble a class in progress. The next day you phone the professor, learn he moved the class to a building closer to his office.

"Didn't you see the note on the chalkboard?" says the gray-voiced man you don't realize is also the mayor of Morgantown.

His tone is condescending, and you don't explain why you didn't see his note. You apologize and make an appointment to pick up the syllabus. Minutes later, deciding this isn't a man you wish to meet, you use the university's convenient auto-mated phone registration system to drop the course from your schedule. You'll take an extra class in the spring, assuming you're still here.

During fifteen-minute breaks in the two classes you don't drop, you chat awkwardly with a few students about the other classes they're taking. Some of them convene after class at a bar called Gibby's, but you decline offers to join them. No one in your classes, save your professors, knows you are visually impaired. Apparently people play pool at this Gibby's, and eventually you might have to explain why you are entirely uninterested in a friendly game of billiards. So many things can go wrong in a bar: losing track of the people you're with while getting your drink, not being able to find the men's room, not knowing when someone is talking to you because the music is so loud and the visual cues of eye contact and reading lips are as useless to you as writing on a chalkboard.

Just when you've come to terms with not making friends, you meet a girl. You met Lana last year, in fact, when she dated Danny. A freshman at the time, she is the very ex who once told him it would require a special girl to date you. Their relationship ended so badly she transferred here after their breakup. Lana is an English major, a smart and talented poet who sits in on your graduate poetry workshop. For a few weeks, the orbit of your small world begins to expand. In late autumn, as you enter the second month of your relationship, Lana leaves you for another graduate student, a chubby Australian who throws lavish, Gatsbyesque parties attended by students as well as professors. This, you decide, is what happens when you talk to people.

The walk to class requires you to cross four streets, none wider than two lanes. The first few times you reach the building safely, you feel a sense of accomplishment, but also ashamed for feeling like you've triumphed over adversity by crossing streets. Prior to this, your solo excursions as a pedestrian consisted of a few inebriated walks home from a fraternity house your senior year of college, a straight line through residential streets you had walked so many times with friends that even after half a dozen Sea Breezes you were confident you could navigate them in the dark. And don't forget that lonely Saturday night senior year when your roommates and everyone else you knew were gone for the weekend. An episode of A&E's *Biography* about Walter Matthau noted that in 1967 the actor won his Academy Award for Best Supporting Actor in a film called *The Fortune Cookie*. From the time the show's narrator uttered those words, you pondered the possibility of Chinese food. Improbably, your college town of six thousand residents had four Chinese restaurants, one of which, you were almost certain, you could reach by crossing only a few streets. You placed your order by phone and, twenty minutes later, carried your food home with the pride of a hunter, a miracle in a plastic bag.

Besides your classroom buildings, your apartment is a safe walk—translation: two-lane streets with stop signs or traffic lights—from several city blocks of stores and restaurants, most of whose identities remain a mystery. The record store to which you made late-night pilgrimages with college friends sits a block and a half from your apartment, and from time to time you ascend the three steps to go inside. You pretend to look for something in the used CDs, browsing long enough for the incense to cling to your shirt.

Some Saturday nights you make your way down High Street, threading a path around queues of undergrads waiting to enter the same clubs you frequented last year while visiting

Rizwan. The two of you had planned to share an apartment this year, but a job at the Centers for Disease Control took him away to Atlanta. Without Riz or Danny or Ron to help define you, you are forced to define yourself. You once thought you were a writer, but that doesn't seem to be the case.

One night, for a few minutes, you join the back of the queue outside the club Elements, breathing in the hairspray and perfume, listening to the drunken laughter of girls who seem so much younger than your twenty-two years. You step out of line, satisfied that you have blended in. These nighttime walks are a new variety of charade; for once, your efforts are less for strangers than for yourself. The sidewalks become the halls of a museum, an installation depicting your hypothetical normal life.

At night, you can see traffic lights amid the dark sky. Fewer cars roam the streets. You study the ones that do, assessing where they go, where they don't, how quickly they accelerate when a signal turns green, whether they yield to pedestrians in the crosswalk. Farther and farther you venture from the home base of your apartment building, circling downtown in wider revolutions, your trip its own destination.

Most days you talk to no one, leaving your apartment only to check your mailbox on the first floor. Geographically, your closest friend is Ron, who lives an hour away in Pittsburgh. Danny lives with his parents twenty miles down the interstate, but you haven't seen him in months. He was not a fan of you dating Lana, and you hadn't been a fan of his increasingly destructive blackout drinking much of your senior year.

Evenings you have class feel lonelier than the evenings you don't leave your apartment. Attempts to engage your class-mates in conversation don't go well. A PhD student seated across the table in African American Narratives, a class of eighteen Caucasian graduate students taught by a white woman in her thirties, seems startled when you join her pre-class banter with another student. The topic is cheese toast. You used to eat cheese toast for breakfast when you were a child, you tell her.

"It's good stuff," says the PhD student in a flat voice. The next week she takes a chair several seats from where you are sitting.

A kitchenette with a three-burner stove and three-quarter-size fridge lines the left wall of your apartment's smaller room. On the right sits the Packard Bell desktop you received the Christmas before your vision loss, which suits your only need: typing papers on the identity politics of Prince's name change to an unpronounceable symbol, ten pages not neces-sarily enhanced by quotations from critical theorists you've been studying.

"Sounds promising," your professor comments on the idea, and you have never heard someone lie less convincingly.

In the corner of the room with the kitchenette, balanced precariously on a TV tray, rest the microwave and toaster oven used for cooking ninety percent of your meals. Next to them sits the two-top dining table that came with the apart-ment, which you use only occasionally, like dental floss and the vacuum, because eating at a table seems like something well-adjusted people do.

Dark as it usually is when you wake up, you never bother opening the blinds. Night after night, you put off bedtime until nine in the morning and wake at 6 p.m., in time to get ready for an evening class.

Saturday nights, once the high-water mark of the college week, are the days you most dread. Now your week revolves around new episodes of professional wrestling, which air on Monday nights. The only shows on TV all weekend are reruns of *Walker, Texas Ranger* and *Touched by an Angel*. Sometimes you draw a bubble bath with dishwashing liquid, John Garabedian's *Open House Party* turned up loud on the clock radio on the back of the toilet. Students at your university have a reputation for rowdy behavior, burning sofas in the streets to commemorate football victories, sometimes losses. West Virginia University is perennially ranked among *Playboy* magazine's top party schools in America, a superlative your quiet apartment does its best to contradict.

Perhaps because the Mountaineers always come up short in big games, perhaps because you've come to equate prosperity with making it out of your home state, you rarely check the football or basketball scores. Even the school's best-known alum, Jerry West, writes in his memoir about a lifelong sense of inferiority, stemming from a humble childhood in the rural hamlet where your grandmother grew up. Despite a career so successful his silhouette still serves as the NBA logo, he remains haunted by eight defeats in the NBA Finals and the last-second missed shot that would have delivered West Virginia its only championship.

Your coffee table grows tall with exit strategies, thick information packets from graduate programs in filmmaking, screenwriting, and something called American Studies. Thanks to your legal blindness, calls to 411 are free of charge, and with no danger of anyone but you stumbling upon your handwriting, you take down the numbers as big as you wish with a felt-tip pen.

Each brochure provides a window to another life. Massachusetts, Illinois, Arizona, California. You could live anywhere. Your skin buzzes with fantasies of alternate lives. The logistics of living in a city and state where you know no one kills much of your buzz, but look at you here, now. How would it be any worse?

You also request information from creative writing programs. Perhaps you simply hadn't applied to enough of them last year. As a psychology major, which you kept as a hedged bet against your writing dreams, one of your textbooks offered different theories of where creativity comes from. Freud believed it was a defense mechanism protecting us against neurosis. Similarly, Jung thought artistic expression came from an intrinsic need to relieve pain or anxiety. It was Alfred Adler's theory, that artists are driven by an inferiority complex, which most resonated with you. It felt even truer when those rejections from MFA programs arrived. Since then you've wondered: Is it really an inferiority complex? If you're not good enough, isn't it simply inferiority?

From time to time, Ron drives seventy-five miles from Pittsburgh and brings you back to his apartment for the weekend. It's two vacations in one: a trip to a major American city as well as a trip to the active, sociable life you might one day live. As you approach Pittsburgh, the Allegheny Tunnel spits the car into a web of metropolitan lights your eyes can almost appreciate.

The Steel City is home to three championship sports franchises, towering buildings, the history of American industry. You pass a street where former World Wrestling Federation champion Bruno Sammartino can be seen mowing his lawn. Ron tells you about a writer named Michael Chabon, who grew up and attended college in Pittsburgh. For years, Ron and his facility with the Internet have introduced you to so many of your favorite movies, bands, even authors, which, you being the one in the master's program in English, feels kind of embarrassing. To you, the Internet remains a far-off ocean in the landlocked state of your life.

Your audiobook library has all of Michael Chabon's books. You request and adore his first novel, *The Mysteries of Pittsburgh*, about a recent college graduate struggling to reconcile who he is with who he wants to be. The next time you visit, Ron points out landmarks from the novel, among them a bookstore fictionalized in an early scene. Inside, standing before the fiction shelves, Ron reads you titles of novels, the jacket copy and blurbs on the back covers, and you shiver as you once did when the subject turned to the short stories you were reading and writing.

Michael Chabon's second novel, *Wonder Boys*, which you loved so completely your eyes welled up at the end, is becoming a movie. Parts of it are being filmed two streets over from Ron's apartment. Answering a flyer, Ron becomes an extra in two scenes. In one of them, he holds a case of beer while standing outside the home of Michael Douglas's character.

"I like the way you hold that beer," Michael Douglas jokes with him between takes.

"I've had a lot of practice," Ron says.

Michael Douglas laughs.

Before your next class, you want to tell this story to one of the people seated near you, but you adhere to your policy of pre-class silence, adopted in the wake of the cheese toast debacle.

You have your own brushes with fame. Weeknights from two until six in the morning, Morgantown's WAJR airs ESPN Radio's *AllNight with Todd Wright*, an irreverent sports talk show with intermittent discussions of pop culture. Each night a few segments present opportunities for listeners to call in. You get through with regularity, a feat that speaks to either your dialing prowess or the paucity of listeners at 4:12 a.m. More than once your clever retorts elicit laughter from Todd Wright—not a chuckle, but a series of full-throated *ha*'s lasting several beats. Your stereo is tuned to the show, the volume all the way down, and as soon as the producer says you're up next, you press RECORD on the stereo's remote. You play your appearances over the phone for Ron, who laughs along with the host. Ron asks why you always say you're calling from Pittsburgh instead of Morgantown. You think you're likelier to get on the air if you say you're calling from a bigger city, you tell him, but the truth is more complicated.

In daylight, you can't rely on headlights and traffic lights to know when it's safe to cross streets. Sometimes other pedestrians are waiting on the curb, and you can cross behind them. The odds are decent that they aren't blind, distracted, or suicidal, but you realize this is a gamble. Party school that this is, it's not beyond the realm of possibility that some students might be drunk or stoned when they step into the crosswalk, even in the afternoon.

News reports of pedestrians being struck and killed by automobiles are not uncommon. Recently Stephen King, while out for a walk, was critically injured by a van. The famous author wears prescription eyeglasses but is not visually impaired. He was not in the road but on the shoulder when the van struck him.

Times when no other pedestrians are waiting to cross a street, you wait for the light to change. You can't see the light turn green, but the stopped cars to your left or right let you know when the signal changes. Beware of two-way streets. Between the yellow lines in the center of the street and the ollie-ollie-oxen-free of the opposite sidewalk lies a void often filled by vehicles wishing to turn. Helpful signals like eye contact or a driver's wave are as useless to you as the walk/don't walk signs you wouldn't be able to see even if they worked, which, you confirm during some nighttime reconnaissance, Morgantown's do not.

There is a third, riskier option. When there are no pedestrians to whom you can pin your safety and no traffic lights or stop signs to part traffic, you can listen for cars. You've used this method for crossing the hilly avenue closest to your own building for months. Cars descending the cobbled pavement of Arnold Street announce themselves with a grinding whirr audible from blocks away. Their warning comes far sooner than the headlights of cars rounding the corner of Willey Street, which runs like a frozen river between your apartment and what looks a lot like a convenience store.

A call to your rental office asking for driving directions to your own building—you're nothing if not resourceful—confirms the nighttime beacon across the street *is*, in fact, a convenience store called Dairy Mart. With no traffic light, no stop sign, and no crosswalk, its fluorescent glow might as well be a desert mirage. There are also no groceries in your apartment, the hundred dollars' worth of canned and packaged items from your parents' last visit more than a month ago reduced to a can of beef stew and three Kraft Singles.

You call Kroger, but the woman who answers seems amused when you ask if they deliver. How much would a taxi cost? You would have to call another to pick you up after you checked out. How would you know which car was the cab? Not all of them are bright yellow. Worse than that, how many people would stare at you in the store, holding item after item a few inches from your face? Finding groceries based largely on your memory of the few times you've been to that Kroger would be, at best, a struggle. Perhaps one of the store's employees could serve as your grocery guide dog, but requesting such help has never been in your wheelhouse. Given the choice between help and not being someone who needs help, you have always preferred the latter.

Meanwhile, a Taj Mahal of beef jerky, chips, Diet Coke, and beer lies a mere fifty feet from your front door. One night, brave with hunger, your checking account shrinking from all your Wendy's meals at the student union, you walk two blocks to the right, your peripheral vision trained on the opposite side of the road. As far as you can tell, there is a sidewalk. As far as you can tell, there are no additional streets to cross, only the parking lot of the bank whose ATM buttons you memorized on the afternoon you moved into your apartment. At the top of High Street, you wait for the glow of a green light against the nighttime sky, confirm traffic is also stopped, and cross the street to Dairy Mart.

The scent of a convenience store, like the library, shopping mall, and airport, teems with limitless choices. Compared to your depleted fridge, the three aisles, freezer case, and wall of beverages feel like the closest you will ever come to infinity. You pick up items from several shelves until you have your bearings in the store. The packaging of most foods, their colors and contours, provides clues to what they are: eggs, milk, ice cream, Campbell's soup. Telling the difference between microwaveable beef stew and ravioli is more than your eyes can manage, but you've learned not to be picky. Desperate as you've been for groceries, you would have been impressed with far less than the offerings of Dairy Mart. Leaving with the aforementioned items as well as three two-liters of Diet Coke, two boxes of cereal—God bless those giant, unchanging cereal logos of your youth—possible granola bars, and a white bag you think your thumb and forefinger have correctly guessed to be Corn Nuts, you carry the heavy bounty three blocks in the opposite direction of your apartment to cross at the traffic light.

After a few trips, you pause at the edge of the Dairy Mart parking lot, tempted by the proximity of your apartment. Twenty feet separate you from the sidewalk in front of the building. You look left. Darkness. You look right. Darkness. You listen left and listen right. Not a sound. Your heart pauses as you step into the road. Time and again, you reach the other side, holding your breath a little less as you come to trust the silence.

When nothing is on TV or the radio, you crank up hip-hop and dance music in your three-disc changer. It's the kind of music—Prince, the Fugees, *Pure Disco* volumes 1 and 2—perfect for an apartment filled with people drinking alcohol, which is to say the soundtrack of your senior year of college. You've tried drinking alone, buying a few six-packs from the Dairy Mart, but all you could think to do with your beer buzz was watch TV. Watching TV sober is less expensive.

Instead of parties, your loud music becomes the soundtrack to your nightly push-ups and dumbbell curls. Exercise is a precautionary measure—hope, some might call it—in the unlikely event a girl in one of your classes ever finds you . . . whatever half a dozen girls in college found you.

One evening, you follow four students with whom you've made occasional small talk into the elevator. Usually you avoid elevators, even the one in your building when you are carrying six bags from Dairy Mart to your fourth-floor apartment, lest someone come around the corner the moment your face is inches from the buttons.

"J.T., are you going to two?" asks the petite, short-haired classmate who once laughed at one of your rare quips before class. She has a kind voice and a boy's first name that somehow adds to her cuteness. Once, before your professor returned from the break, the two of you questioned the usefulness of the esoteric articles assigned with each novel. Another time she told you she is in the master's program because she couldn't think of anything else to do with her life.

Indeed, you are going to the second floor. These three students hang out, you've gathered, but overheard conversations suggest they don't know one another especially well, passengers on an airplane who will go their separate ways when their flight taxis to the gate. Would it be so terrible, you often wonder, to have some placeholder friends?

"I love your coat," says the girl with the boy's name, feeling your corduroy arm.

I'm a slave to fashion, you'll wish you had said in a few hours. Oh, this old thing? For days, glib line after glib line will present themselves to you, responses not particularly clever, but lines that might have made the girl with the boy's name smile, blossomed into conversation, an invitation to hang out sometime and become one of these people who have people to talk to after class.

"Thanks," you say.

The elevator opens. You and your classmates exit the building through different doors, and you walk home alone through lightly falling snow.

———

As long as it's been since you've kissed someone, 2 a.m. commercials for *Girls Gone Wild* videos and phone sex hotlines seem to speak directly to you. Rates of $2.99 per minute aren't in your budget, but an ad for a Pittsburgh singles line claims calls are free except for any long-distance rates that may apply. The next time the ad comes on, you rush to your thirteen-inch TV and manage to jot down the phone number before it disappears.

"Welcome to Lavalife, the place where singles mingle." The prerecorded voice of the woman in your ear is flirtatious and warm, a wink in her words that seems to say, Stay right here, cutie, I'm going to go get us a couple of drinks.

A more formal message reassures you the call is free but long-distance charges may apply. After this, the business-toned voice instructs you how to set up your own profile and account. The voice remains tempting, but it's the voice of a woman not yet ready for the weekend, a lady who has a job, and when that job is done, well, maybe then we'll see about those drinks.

"To skip these steps and get right down to the action," says the voice, slipping back into her bedroom timbre, "press 1."

You press 1. You have no intention of setting up a profile, but listening to greetings is free, save those long-distance charges.

"Male callers, press 1."

You press 1.

"To listen to ads for those seeking love and steady relationships, press 1."

Let's hear what the other options are.

"For dating and casual relationships, press 2. For intimate

encounters, press 3. For the wild side, press 4. Couples and swingers, press 5."

You think it over.

"Are you still there? You didn't make a choice in the time allotted."

The options repeat, and you go with intimate encounters.

Most messages are brief, coy if not shy. Some are more confident, self-possessed, quite graphic in what these ladies of the greater Pittsburgh area would do with you—to you—were you in the same room. As much as an average day demands of your imagination, you're thankful for how little some of these greetings leave to that overworked part of your brain.

The color and shape of a woman's eyes can't be heard, but a voice lets you know if she'll look you in the eyes while she's talking. Once in a while you're convinced you can hear, in the narrow nook of a syllable, what a girl's hand would feel like inside yours, the number of seconds before your joined hands would become humid with shared heat, whether she would be the first to say she loves you or wait to see if you said it first.

Some nights you grow tired of intimate encounters and switch to romance and steady relationships. "I just want somebody I can be myself around," says a girl from the Pittsburgh neighborhood of Squirrel Hill. "I'm looking for somebody who's fun," says another, biting down on the word *fun* in a way that conveys what a stick-in-the-mud her ex must have been. They want guys who are *super kind*, who will be their *best friend*, who *like to do things, you know?* Maybe you are all of these things. Maybe you are none of these things. As vividly as you can picture these girls' faces, you have trouble imagining yourself beside them, dating them, making them happy.

In addition to twenty-five books for your classes each semester, you plow through dozens more over the summer. "Reading is a great escape!" said Bugs Bunny or Donald Duck on a library poster from your youth. Once a week you phone the state library for the blind and physically handicapped to request new books. For the first time, you ask for a novel you've already read. *Martin Eden* is Jack London's story of a rough-hewn sailor who falls for an upper-class girl and, in an effort to win her love, teaches himself to become a writer. The first time you read it, a few months after your diagnosis, you found inspiration in Martin's improbable journey from working-class nobody to world-renowned author. This time it's the novel's sad ending that resonates. Martin finds unprecedented literary success, but only after Ruth has ended their relationship, pleading with him to get a stable job. The love of a Ruth does not await you on the other side of inertia and uncertainty. Neither do you possess the lifetime's worth of seafaring voyages and Klondike expeditions Jack London had amassed before the age you are now. What have you ever done that anyone would want to read about?

Yet you continue to write. In recent months, you've penned short stories about a professional wrestler, a mysterious musician who is obviously a stand-in for Prince, a woman who thinks she sees a man fall from an airplane. They're assignments for creative writing, the only class in this program you haven't considered skipping each and every week. The professor, a diminutive, maternal, exceedingly well-read woman in her fifties whose book of short stories won a major prize, believes a couple of your stories are good enough to send to literary journals. Pleased as you are when she recommends you pursue an MFA, you heard this before as an undergraduate. Fool me twice, you think.

Yet you continue to write. Late into the night, you hold your microcassette recorder inches from your face, rewinding and erasing until the sentences sound right in your ear. You don't know if they will sound right to anyone else, but you keep going. And in the end, it's because you don't know why you keep writing that makes it seem like you should keep writing.

Worries about where you'll be next year grow by the day. You also fear that your modest strides toward independence won't travel with you to a new town. Your spartan diet of eggs, cereal, and canned soup isn't a menu you'd like to continue deep into your twenties, but for nearly a year you've obtained these groceries without assistance. Armed only with directions you received over the phone, you found a place to get your hair cut—even if the student stylists at the beauty school haven't been the most consistent stewards of your sideburns and left part. It's the terror of starting over, of once again having to rely on others, that compels you to place a call to student disability services.

It's a stab in the dark, but you're curious if technology has come any farther from where it was a few years ago.

Your sophomore year of college, the director of the Learning Center led you to what seemed to be a storage closet. With the flourish of a magician's big reveal, the elderly, hunchbacked woman showed you a computer with several components attached, an ungainly setup a 1970s police chief might refer to as the mainframe. She pressed a few buttons on the keyboard, clicked the mouse. HAL 9000 began to read in a slow, cadence-free voice more primitive than the narrator of your talking dictionary. It took you a full minute to recognize the passage as content from your textbook for biological psychology. After futile hours trying to decipher the mispronounced names of neurotransmitters, you pleaded for the return of your human reader.

Your prior interactions with this university's disability services didn't go well. The meeting with the director while you were in high school, the one who advised you to aim for a report card of straight C's, dissuaded you from coming here as an undergrad. More recently, at the start of this master's program, the office gave you a referral to a student reader for the handouts and books you couldn't obtain on cassette. The second week of the semester, the girl with whom they put you in touch phoned to say she was super stressed with her own classes and wouldn't be able to get your reading done that week, leaving you to read twelve pages of poems with your magnifier, word by word, letter by letter. In class, you had a lot more to say about the shorter ones. The Bible-thin pages of your critical theory compendium, the font not quite as large as the ingredients on a pack of chewing gum, went unread.

Three semesters later, you're counting doors in an unfamiliar building until you reach the office of the cheerful woman you've spoken to on the phone. Her detailed directions suggest she's used to students with less sight than you have.

"Technology's come a long way just in the last few years," says the orange-haired woman, who reminds you of a young Mrs. Garrett from *The Facts of Life*. Often when someone knows about your disability before you meet, their warmth is layered with condescension, but not this woman.

She leads you down the hall to a small computer lab, into a corner partitioned from the other computers. While the desktop boots, she hands you headphones and puts on a pair herself. Moments later, a digital voice says, "JAWS for Windows is ready."

The voice of JAWS—Job Access With Speech—reads you what is on the screen, including menus to any Windows-based program. The enunciation and vocal quality are more advanced than your talking dictionary and clock. Young Mrs. Garrett shows you how to adjust the speed, tone, and volume. She closes the window and opens a blank document in Microsoft Word, asks you to type something.

The keys you press echo in your ear. She demonstrates how buttons on the number pad control what JAWS reads.

"Pretty easy, isn't it?"

Overwhelmed by everything you can suddenly do, you have to clear your throat before you answer. "It is."

She opens Internet Explorer. Bursts of color appear on the monitor. JAWS confirms the page has loaded, and the wonder you feel upon visiting your first website rivals your first turn of a car's ignition. The new millennium is weeks old, and you are finally on the World Wide Web, if only the university's home page.

JAWS occasionally hiccups when a page loads, and sites with intricate graphics, you'll discover, don't seem to load in their entirety. Still, the last time you used a modem the term *Internet* hadn't been coined and it took eight and a half hours for a friend to send you a compressed file containing a photo of a topless woman you were ninety percent certain was not Kathy Ireland.

In the coming weeks, you'll devour pop culture trivia with the hunger of a shipwrecked sailor, conduct your own research for a paper for the first time since eleventh grade, learn the correct spelling of book titles and author names it turns out your library has after all. Right now the woman has another program she wants to show you.

Paired with a scanner, this software translates printed pages into a digitized voice similar to the screen reader. You're currently on your fifth human reader in a year, and the uncertainty of who and how reliable the next one will be is a constant source of anxiety.

The program's accuracy depends, among other factors, on how hard your hand presses the spine during scanning. Some serif fonts it seems to regard as obscure dialects of a dead language. Waiting up to a minute for two pages to scan makes scanning two out-of-print Irish novels for one of your classes a cumbersome process, but the reward of reading a book on your own far outweighs the hassle. That reading some of your books requires a fifteen-minute walk doesn't bother you in the least. It's nice to leave your apartment with a purpose, to have somewhere to go.

The first acceptance comes on a Friday afternoon. It's a younger MFA program in Texas your thesis adviser recommended you apply to, in part as a safety school. After a few minutes, the program's director puts a National Book Award–winning novelist on the line to make a personalized pitch.

How many hours would it take to drive to Texas? To fly? From the photograph of what might be a sun-dappled river in the brochure, you get no sense of how prevalent sidewalks are in the town, or if housing options near the school are also near convenience stores. These are not questions you want to ask the program director or the National Book Award winner. Your mom, helping you with applications, asked if you wanted to check the box for disabled. You declined, not wanting your limitations to be a factor in the school's decision.

You choose a small school in Virginia, the most competitive program that accepted you. It isn't an MFA but a one-year master's program with a long list of distinguished alumni. It's a small woman's college with coed graduate programs, and the lack of housing near campus compels you to mention your low vision to the program director in your second email. Initially it doesn't look hopeful—no apartments within walking distance as far as he knows, no on-campus housing, he'll have to check on bus routes—but his assistant writes back later in the week with a lead on a trailer half a mile from campus.

For only $285 a month, your well-maintained trailer has central air, a washer and dryer, a full bath, two bedrooms, and a back deck with a privacy fence. Your landlords, a woodworker and a librarian, live next door with their young daughter. The first floor of their home is a store selling his hand-crafted furniture. Wonder of wonders, two hundred feet up the road sits a gas station and convenience store.

There is no sidewalk on the street leading to your trailer. Nor does a sidewalk run along the four-lane road—an ostensible highway—leading to the college.

A grassy shoulder provides a buffer from traffic. On the half-mile walk to campus, cars rush toward you, the tailwind ruffling your hair in the weeks before hair gel will mark the first revision to your hairstyle since a spiky experiment in fourth grade. For part of the way, orange construction barrels provide another barrier, if not exactly protection. Each zooming vehicle is your natural predator deciding capriciously not to eat you. Eventually, you trust they are not going to veer off the road the way that van did with Stephen King, but a fear of that happening leaves the trailer with you every morning.

Halfway to campus, the mostly flat shoulder becomes a sidewalk, and the only street you cross before the entrance to the college is a residential road onto which you never see cars turn. You don't even have to cross the busy four-lane because a pedestrian tunnel underneath it leads to the college on the other side.

Convenient as it is, the tunnel is a longer walk than simply crossing the four-lane road to the college's main entrance. From time to time, you regard the other side the way a child eyes the bright contents of a toy store window. Someday, you think. There *is* a traffic light. Last year you crossed streets with traffic lights all the time. Some contained three or four lanes, even if they were one-way streets. Time after time, you watch cars on this four-lane come to a stop, the crosswalk parting before you like a biblical body of water. Each time you pass it by for the prudent safety of the tunnel.

One gray day, you're running late for your morning class. Emboldened by the lack of glaring sun, you pause on the curb and assess the cars on the other side of the four-lane road. They come to a stop. Your ears, so useful in crossing the dark and empty streets near your last apartment, are no help in this scenario. To your left, there is only open road, and you decide this will be the day you trade your tortoise shell for the confidence of the fabled hare. You step quickly off the curb and are ten feet into your journey when the sharp, sustained note of a car horn punches a hole in the morning.

Another dozen feet separate you from the concrete median. Your legs propel you forward, but you move in slow motion, your heart a bass drum echoing in your ears. Your life does not flash before you. Your mind empties. There is only a two-dimensional image of the ground, the stopped cars on the other side of the median, the vague impression of grass on the far side of them—all of it flattened by the hammer of the still-blasting horn. There is no time to run; you can only push off from the ground, one final shove of your feet carrying you onto the concrete island of the rest of your life.

The horn fades in the distance. You remain on the median while the stopped cars in front of you begin to move, right to left. Another light cycle comes and goes before you trust the pattern in which they speed away, before you trust time itself.

Eventually, the cars remain stationary long enough for you to believe you can reach the other side. Only when your unsteady legs ascend the steps to the building where you have class does it make sense, how one side of the street could be stopped and the other not: The turn lane had a green arrow. This epiphany, the how and why of your almost death, brings you no solace.

For hours, days, the sound of the car horn scores your thoughts, your heart vaporizing in Pavlovian response to the unfading memory. You wish they were nightmares you could leave behind in bed each morning, but your dreams rarely dwell on the negative. Your dreams, in fact, seem to mock your waking fears and anxieties, constructing carefree narratives in which you make out with Madonna, Jennie Garth, and for reasons you can't explain, Bette Midler, who turns out to be an incredible kisser. If these dreams are the efforts of your subconscious to process a near-death experience, they don't reduce the panic in your chest when you leave your trailer on foot every morning.

The lesson seems obvious enough: Do not cross a street without absolute certainty that every lane of traffic is stopped and will remain that way for the period of time required for you to reach the other side. Finding meaning in the fact that you were almost hit by a car going between thirty-five and fifty miles an hour is more difficult. Everything happens for a reason, people liked to tell you when your vision began to go. You wanted to believe them, but there's a fine line between looking for a reason and blaming yourself for going blind.

If your English classes taught you anything, it's that meaning can rest in the smallest details, in every moment and gesture and line of dialogue. What if, say, your impaired vision, in grand metaphorical tradition, lends you an ability to see what others don't? It's pretty to think so, but you are not a character in a novel, and the only meaning you find in almost being killed, no matter how deeply you scrutinize the event, is that you are still alive.

Attempts to turn your trailer into the sullen bunker your last apartment became fail within a few weeks. There are sixteen students in the program, and most evenings a group gathers at someone's apartment to hang out. Close as you all become, your low vision is known to most in short order. Your reluctance to accept rides is challenged early on as unreasonable, stubborn. Are writers this perceptive or have you always been this transparent?

You're far from the most talented writer in the program— one of your classmates published a collection of short stories with a major press last summer—but you never feel as though you don't belong here. Screen-reading software and a refurbished scanner mean you can read everything for your classes without relying on another person. For years, your primary strategy of revision involved spell-checking and a few line edits suggested by a professor, provided you could locate the lines in question. Now your computer can navigate any portion of a document with simple keystrokes. Actual editing—finding and selecting, deleting and pasting, rewriting and rewriting and rewriting—feels like the power to fly.

Between a novel in progress and numerous short stories, you write more than twenty pages per week. For the first time, you send out two of your stories to literary journals. Their comprehensive rejection might sting more if you didn't notice how dramatically your writing seems to be improving. How much are you improving? Not as much as you think, it seems, when that spring the rejections to MFA programs begin their annual migration to your mailbox.

An eleventh-hour acceptance to a school in North Carolina, a program that rejected you two times in the past, saves you from moving back into your parents' house. A teaching assistantship means financial independence—no more help from your parents, no more checks from Social Security. An annual salary of nine thousand dollars feels like you've won the lottery. Most of all, you're relieved to have two more years to get better as a writer, even if it means a fourth and fifth year in graduate school and a third master's degree in the same subject.

"He's found something he's good at," your mother tells an aunt over the phone. Does she mean writing or graduate school?

Early on, the most difficult aspect of teaching is filling fifty minutes three days a week. A class size of twenty makes learning voices a simple affair, and a compact classroom allows for credible eye contact. On the first day, you instruct students not to raise their hands when they wish to speak. Your chalkboard penmanship won't get you gigs addressing wedding invitations, but neither is it illegible.

Grading papers is more tedious than you anticipated. Before you can read them, you remove the staples with your fingernails and scan each page of every essay into your com-

puter. At first you try marking passages the way your own
professors have always done. Holding the paper under a lamp,
your magnifier against the edge of the page, you scrawl mini-
mal comments in the margin. That students might not be able
to read your handwriting doesn't occur to you until one of
them asks what you've written. You stare at the page she's
holding, not about to take out your magnifier. Even if you
did, you wouldn't be able to read your note any better than
she can.

"Sorry. I'll try to write neater next time."

As much as you wish to hide your disability from students,
you also want to be an effective teacher. Your supervisor, the
director of composition, is aware of your low vision. She shares
with you her own grading philosophy, one with a basis in well-
researched pedagogy. She has not written on a student essay in
decades. Instead, she types her comments on a separate sheet.
Any grammatical issues can be referenced in your comments,
but students, she asserts, need to understand the difference
between *correction* and *revision*. You don't know about all that,
as they say, but you've put handwritten comments on your last
paper.

When your supervisor observes your class, she asks if
you noticed the girl in the front row doing math homework.
What about the fellow napping in the back? Blood rushes to
your face. Embarrassed as you are, you also feel vindicated
for not telling these eighteen-year-olds about your impaired
vision. How many of them would be asleep or doing homework for other classes if they knew you wouldn't notice?
Would cashiers give you the correct change if they knew you

wouldn't check the bills they handed you until you sorted them into different compartments of your wallet when you got home? Would the average stranger regard you with the same pity as the attractive flight attendant you once asked for assistance during a changeover, who after you explained your poor eyesight said, "You have beautiful eyes," in a tone consistent with *what a shame?*

The end of another master's program approaches, and the requirement to read your work in front of an audience produces a tumescent ball of anxiety in your stomach. Your writing teachers, aware of your situation, always called on one of your classmates to read a sample from your stories that were up for discussion, sometimes skipping this perfunctory exercise altogether. In your first program, you went to great lengths to memorize a page and a half of prose until one horrifying evening the final few paragraphs took the last train to Forgetsville. You feigned a tickle in the back of your throat until the professor took over. As an undergraduate, your thesis reading consisted of you sitting in the audience of professors and fellow readers while Danny read your interminable, twenty-one-page short story. If you were to ask the director of the MFA program, you suspect he would allow someone to read your work for you, if not waive this degree requirement entirely, but you've grown weary of acknowledging your limitations. Also, you have an idea.

Thanks to your screen reader, you stopped dictating first drafts into a microcassette recorder a couple of years ago.

Now you type them on the computer, editing as you go. The digital voice of your desktop travels from ears to brain, landing in your throat as your own voice calibrates the rhythm of sentences. If you slow the screen reader down, you can almost catch up to the words in a real-time facsimile of reading.

You practice "reading" while Meredith is at work, pacing the bedroom you've shared for nearly a year. A poet who graduated from the program last May, your girlfriend has no idea how terrified you are of making a fool of yourself. As is your wont in relationships, you've tried hard to show your low vision is no big deal, and a successful thesis reading would go a long way toward proving this.

With your reading two weeks away, backing out is no longer an option. You manage no more than two sentences in a row without stumbling over words. You should have started practicing much sooner. Why are all your sentences so long? Line by line, you translate the digital voice in your ears into poorly inflected sentences, translating the first audio draft into another, better-inflected draft on a second tape. Take after take, the quality of your "reading" improves until you've rehearsed so many times you might have the two chapters memorized.

The evening of the reading you come close to throwing up. A glass of wine doesn't help; ditto the double shot of Pepto and Diet Coke, whose carbonation you flatten with a fork. Thesis readings are formal events on the campus calendar, five Friday nights scattered between February and April, two readers each. Applause after you're introduced sounds far away.

The audience is an amorphous collection of bodies in couches and chairs, the room filled to capacity. This is the one thing your eyes do well: blurring what you'd rather not see. You can, however, make out the latecomers forced to stand, several others seated on the floor.

People laugh sympathetically when you confess how nervous you are. They have no reason to think your anxiety is anything more than a run-of-the-mill fear of public speaking. The public speaking you don't have a problem with. It's the standing before a room of seventy-five people, half of them strangers, and trying to conceal your inability to read that makes you light-headed.

Typically, thesis readers preface their reading with a list of thank-yous, and yours, thanks to nerves, forgets to include Meredith, seated on the sofa five feet from the lectern. Without explanation, you don the earbuds. You take a deep breath and fix your gaze on the two chapters you've printed and placed on the lectern. They're of no use to you, but they make for a convincing prop.

You press PLAY. Your own calm voice fills your ears. The first few sentences under your belt, sensation returns to your body. The prerecorded words are a quarter second ahead of the words in your mouth, a tenuous tightrope, but you navigate all five pages of chapter one without a single mistake.

Pausing for a sip of water, you continue with chapter two, unfazed by the laughter that comes at the lines you hoped were funny. Afterward, praise for your novel, a romantic comedy set in the world of professional wrestling, is effusive and seemingly sincere. People ask Meredith why she was laughing louder than anyone—hadn't she heard you practice reading a hundred times?

Not one person asks about the earbuds. No one inquires about the moment midway through the second chapter when you tripped over a sentence and had to rewind. Congratulations. You fooled them all.

7

TOO LONG TO
STOP NOW

WE MET IN A class called Structure of Fiction. On the first day, the professor had us introduce ourselves by offering an interpretation of the course title. I defined structure as the choices a writer makes. A few students later, the second-year poet named Meredith with long, dark hair quoted part of my answer in hers. Her name sounded familiar. More than a week would go by, including a group bowling outing, a gathering of MFA students at Old Town Draught House after Thursday workshop, and a pair of lengthening phone conversations that began as simple invitations, before I remembered where I had heard her name: Meredith was the one with the boyfriend in Tokyo.

But I could be wrong.

In Meredith's version, our first meeting was at her apartment for a game of Scattergories, a board game requiring handwritten answers on slips of paper no larger than movie tickets. I had met her roommate, Joanna, during orientation for teaching assistants. Nearly everyone in the program rented apartments within walking distance of one another in the College Hill neighborhood. Directly across the street from me lived the writer in my fiction class named Matt, who had become, in a span of a few weeks, the best friend I had made since college. As gregarious as he was introspective, Matt was the one who suggested we head over to Meredith and Joanna's.

If I had known we would be playing board games, I would have dragged my feet a little harder. The second season of CBS's *Big Brother* was building toward an exciting conclusion, and three episodes a week kept me pretty busy. The problems with board games for someone with low vision are legion. Even a basic question-and-answer game like Trivial Pursuit, of which I owned three versions, requires seeing the six-sided die and which color rectangles lie in either direction. That and the questions must be read by other players. Close as I was to Matt and another fiction writer named Jenny, who also had been in my writing program in Virginia and felt like the big sister I always wished for, the students here didn't gel as instantly as we had at my last school. As usual, I was in no hurry to debrief the masses on what I couldn't do, and my strides toward openness the previous year were looking like the product of others drawing me out of my shell more than personal growth.

Seven of us formed a loose circle in the small living room.

Meredith returned from the kitchen with brownies. When she held the plate in front of me, I held up a hand.

"Are you sure?"

"Yeah, I'm good. Thanks, though."

So many things can go wrong when reaching for food, including but not limited to my thumb and forefinger landing in the wrong section of the plate; touching, defacing, or possibly knocking onto the floor a brownie or precariously arranged cheese on a cracker, or, the Grand Guignol of canapés, a chip that must be sent on a recon mission into a dip of unknown depth or viscosity. There is also the matter of where I have to direct my gaze in order to align my clearest peripheral vision with the plate in front of me. How many women over the years have taken silent umbrage at what must look like a long, meaningful look at their breasts? Thus, no matter how hungry I was or how inviting what I was being offered, no matter how much more people like you when you eat their food at a party, I always passed.

Pencils and paper made their way around the room. I had two choices: decline to play this game or explain that I would not be able to play this game. The former, never a crowd-pleaser, can come across as aggressively antisocial in smaller groups. These were people I'd be around for the next year or two, so I blurted out that I had blind spots that made it too hard to write my answers on the little blanks provided. I took great care with my phrasing. Too hard. Never impossible. Not once had I ever said I can't drive; it was always I don't drive, which wasn't a lie. I didn't drive. If that particular verb left room for one to infer choice, so be it.

"Who has spots?" asked a tipsy poet from Mississippi.

I raised my hand, wishing I too were drinking, but Matt and I were recovering from too many pale ales the night before.

"Let's play on teams," someone suggested, and everyone's eagerness to get on with the game—and attention spans shortened by alcohol—excused me from elaborating on my low vision.

Because we were seated next to each other, Meredith and I formed a team. She moved her chair closer to mine. She seemed like someone whose parents made her befriend new kids in school, invite them home for dinner. My guess wasn't far off. Meredith was, I would learn, from a family of Mormons, and although she had abandoned the religion in college, she was a direct descendant of the church's third president, her relatives prominent politicians in the state of Utah.

Our partnership began poorly. Meredith must have been in the kitchen when I explained the limitations of my eyes. When I told her I couldn't see the card, she leaned closer. I appreciated the proximity to her recently washed hair—Vidal Sassoon was one of my favorite scents of women's shampoo— but the extra inches between my eyes and the slip of paper helped about as much as increasing a 12-point font to 13.

"Could you tell me what categories are on the paper?" I said.

"Okaaay," she said, stretching out the word. This struck her as even stranger than turning down brownies.

The next round she leaned in close again, treating my request for her to read the categories as a onetime deal.

Tired of explaining that I couldn't see the paper, I stopped helping. Eventually, she stopped leaning. Within the hour, the game devolved, as board games will when most participants are drinking.

"He was such a cold fish," Meredith would recall years later, telling our origin story to a new acquaintance. In her wedding toast, Meredith's maid of honor would go so far as to compare me to Mr. Darcy, whose introduction to Elizabeth Bennett goes so poorly that Jane Austen's original title for *Pride and Prejudice* had been *First Impressions*. This tale of wrongly judged book covers became our mythology. It wasn't quite how I remembered it, but Meredith's version made for a better toast.

Neither of us was wrong. Memory chooses which stories we tell, and memory can be an unreliable narrator. There are also the parts of stories we try to forget. We always left out, for example, that while we were falling in love Meredith was still dating a man she planned to marry.

They had met in Prague while teaching English to Czech students. If that didn't sound enough like an Ethan Hawke movie, he was a British guy about to start graduate school in linguistics. Last summer they had lived together in Tokyo, where they both taught English as a second language. Meredith told me this after class, over glasses of orange juice at her kitchen table.

By now she was aware of my blind spots. It sank in during bowling when, seated next to her once again, I asked her which pins remained standing after my first ball. If the tone in which I described the failure of my optic nerves vacillated between glib and detached, it was the same way, the only way, I had been telling the story for nearly a decade.

Lengthening phone calls progressed to Meredith's daily pop-ins to my cubicle in the TA offices, down the hall from where she worked as an editor on the literary journal. Midnight conversations over orange juice became Saturday night viewings of Kubrick and Aronofsky films. When I complained about my back during class, her offer to give me a massage seemed completely innocent—at parties, Meredith was the girl who gave out back rubs, and that, too, seemed completely innocent because everyone knew she had a boyfriend. I don't know if the future linguist would approve of his future wife trading weekly massages in a dimly lit apartment while Chris Isaak and Prince serenaded us on my stereo, but he wasn't here and I was. Even when Meredith asked if I'd mind if she took off her bra—It's just my back, it's not like you're seeing anything—it seemed like no big deal. After all, I had been taking my shirt off.

Oddly, it was the night we caressed each other's hands for hours on my futon, fully clothed, when it became clear what we had been doing. The third CD in my three-disc changer had come to a stop. Meredith rose up to leave. I laid a hand on her shoulder.

"You don't have to go," I said.

Without a word, Meredith lay back down.

In the weeks and months that followed, as we tried to make sense of our own unfolding narrative, Meredith would describe a palpable electricity when my hand touched her shoulder. It's true that currents run through the skin, but it's more than simple sensation. We communicate through touch, the electricity transmitting what we're incapable of saying with words. If we had rationalized all our weeks of post-class massages as the kinds of things friends *say* to one another, there was no mistaking what we said for those few hours, tracing the contours of each other's palms. Our fingertips migrated to each other's hairlines but nowhere else. The messages, echoing in every exhalation, weren't hard to interpret.

We didn't call each other for several days. In class, we sat in our usual adjacent seats, but during the break a consistent buffer of two or three classmates remained between us. Nevertheless, we found ourselves side by side as we left the building, side by side on the mild incline of College Hill.

"I'm hungry," Meredith said.

"I have Pop-Tarts," I must have said. If it wasn't Pop-Tarts, it would have been Pizza Rolls or mozzarella sticks.

"I could go for a Pop-Tart," she said.

We ate Pop-Tarts in my living room, memories of a few nights ago humming in the silence.

"So Friday night . . ." she said, pausing to let me finish her thought.

"Friday night," I said, tossing that hot potato right back to her.

"Did that really happen?"

By now we sat on the futon, still in its couch position.

"What do you remember happening?" I hoped my noncommittal responses came across as flirty and coy and not as the timid replies of someone terrified of making a false step.

"I don't want to hurt you," Meredith whispered.

"Don't worry about me," I said, and if our horizontal positions on the futon and the half inch between our noses were any indication, at least one of us bought my false bravado.

We kissed. And kissed. And kissed.

"God, you are so attractive," she said.

God, you are so wrong, I thought, but somehow I believed her.

The boyfriend remained a boyfriend, halfway around the world but hardly out of mind. I was the one she wanted to be with, she kept reminding me, but winter break came and went and she hadn't yet broken up with him. When she finally did so in late January, she was surprised that I was surprised. Had I really seemed so confident?

She asked me for some time to grieve the relationship, to put space between their ending and our beginning. It seemed like emotional sleight of hand since we had begun months ago, but I told her to take as much time as she needed. The next night she asked if she could come over.

"I had to see you." In serious moments, Meredith paused between words, choosing them as carefully as a poet. "I needed to know if the person who could hurt someone so badly is the same person who can also love you so much."

"Is she?"

"I hope so."

Writing a novel was harder than I thought it would be. Each morning, I sat down at the computer and tried to be productive. I didn't make coffee until Meredith left for work.

She hated the smell, a disdain she claimed had nothing to do with her caffeine-free Mormon upbringing. More than my coffee, she hated mornings, a feeling enhanced by where she was working.

The MFA in creative writing has never been the most versatile degree. Sharper critics of the increasingly ubiquitous programs argue it doesn't even prepare you to be a writer. In a well-circulated story, a class of graduating poets asked their Pulitzer Prize–winning teacher what they might do for jobs after graduation. "You could always," he said with no apparent irony, "just be poets."

With undergraduate student loans, her share of rent, and monthly payments for a pre-owned Mazda I helped her purchase, Meredith struggled to be a poet. She didn't want to teach, but other word-related fields like editing and grant writing, even proofreading, proved tough to break into. Thus, in June, on the cusp of my third month of handling all our expenses while I also wasn't getting paid during the summer, Meredith began commuting forty minutes five days a week to do data entry at a paint factory.

My novel was about a small-town copy editor who accidentally befriends a famous professional wrestler modeled on a cross between the Rock and Prince. Despite its resurgence in popularity, no one had yet written the great American wrestling novel. By summer's end, I had all of two and a half chapters, but they felt good, like something I wanted to finish. "Keep going with this," said one of my professors when I showed him the first hundred pages. "I think it has commercial appeal," said his typed comments, "and I mean that in the best way." This was a writer whose work was a big reason I wanted to attend this program. His comments on my short stories had been kind but restrained, which lent even more weight to his praise of the novel.

By summer's end, Meredith traded the paint factory for an administrative position at a nonprofit that would eventually provide benefits and a salary of twenty-seven thousand dollars, three times what I would make as fiction editor of the university's literary journal. A five-minute commute made her no less tired at the end of a nine-hour workday, and after a few weeks at the new job she asked if I could start cooking dinner. Since moving in with me, Meredith had been preparing all our dinners. My dad had done most of the cooking when I was growing up, but after my many years of Croissant Pockets and Pasta Roni, it took me a while to warm to the idea. It took even longer to make something worthy of a compliment. At the same time, I was surprised how little sight cooking required. Taste proved far more important. It was laziness and inertia, not blindness, that had limited my menu.

When I lived alone, I had washed my clothes at Jenny's house or in the basement of Matt's apartment across the street. With twice the laundry, Meredith and I opted for the laundromat, an increasingly fraught pair of hours every other week during which I came to understand the letters FBS in her email address. While meeting her college friends in Virginia, I asked them to tell me what it stood for. Meredith begged them not to, laughing but also maybe not joking.

"Flaming Ball of Stress," they said, and broke into laughter.

"Now you know," Meredith said, patting me on the knee.

Growing up as the middle of three daughters, Meredith had an upper-middle-class childhood with an attorney for a father. Then one day her father's boss committed suicide. Meredith's father started his own practice, but his income sank under the weight of his bighearted willingness to let payments slide, trading legal hours for cases of cereal or yard work, sometimes working for free. A back injury and the arrival of three more children prevented Meredith's mother from working. Most of the daily responsibilities involved in raising the younger siblings fell to Meredith and her older sister, which is how a poet in her mid-twenties came to approach domestic chores as though her life depended on them.

For a time, I could pretend Meredith and I were any couple in the laundromat, mutually frustrated by the scarcity of washing machines, the slowness of dryers, the absurdity of a laundromat in the South without air-conditioning. No one loves cleaning, so it seemed unremarkable for our moods to grow overcast while we were scrubbing sinks and floors.

My friends never seemed to mind the supermarket as much as my girlfriends, but every time Meredith and I went, there were so many people, so many carts we had to squeeze past, so many items we couldn't find with only one of us able to look. Within weeks of our shopping together, the supermarket had become the same crucible in which my last serious relationship crumbled.

"What kind of cookies do you want?" Meredith asked, a thousand boxes and bags spanning both sides of the aisle.

"Do they have anything with peanut butter?"

This was the kind of open-ended question I tried not

to ask. Meredith's sighs and sullen moods by the time we checked out, no matter how efficiently I had organized our list by every item's location in the store, justified my guilt for these queries.

"I don't see anything with peanut butter."

"What about Nutter Butters?"

"What are Nutter Butters?"

I described the peanut-shaped sandwich cookies, trying to remember the last time I'd had them. Did they still make Nutter Butters? Sensing Meredith's mood beginning to shift, I reached for what felt like a bag of Chips Ahoy! and placed it in the cart.

Within months of Meredith finishing her MFA, her first poems were accepted for publication. She had submitted to ten literary journals, and half of them wanted to publish her work. Having received only form rejections when I sent out my stories, I knew how rare an acceptance was, let alone five in the span of weeks.

"Oh my God," Meredith said, opening one of the envelopes after work. The editor was a poet whose collections she owned.

I picked her up, kissed her, spun her half a turn. "You're going to be a famous poet."

Meredith's smile faded quickly. "Don't say that."

"I just mean—"

"Just stop."

Her protest seemed strong, but I was enough of a sports fan to believe in jinxes and the perils of overconfidence.

The harshness of her reaction also reminded me of our first argument the previous summer. It was one of those thick southern days when you wish it would just get on with it and rain, but the best you ever get is a few hours of cloud cover. I couldn't tell if Meredith's dour mood was caused by boredom or sadness. When I suggested she try writing, it was the first time I had seen her angry.

"Seriously. Why don't you write anymore?" I said.

"I don't know. Maybe because I'm exhausted?"

I had taken over the cooking, but I was no help at the grocery store. Every time we needed milk, shampoo, Sudafed, Palmolive, Windex, bread, garlic, hand soap, linguini, bananas, peanut butter, paper towels, toilet paper, napkins, Kleenex, Meredith had to drive. Meredith had to read the list, find each item on the shelf, push buttons on the card reader at the register, nothing for me to do but lift the bags from cart to car and carry them inside.

At the laundromat, I carried our overflowing baskets from washer to dryer, folded at a feverish pace to make sure I was doing more than my share, but when the time came to set the cycle on the washer and adjust the dryer temperature, I could only watch.

When cleaning the floors, no matter how many times I cast the Swiffer and broom into the corner behind the door, no matter how vigorously I scrubbed the ledge of the bathtub—so hard my arms and back ached for days—there was always some obstinate spot of mold, some elusive tumbleweed of hair and dust Meredith had to take care of.

———

When we moved into a middle unit of a small apartment complex in the spring, I was hopeful that we had solved our domestic problems. My parents bought us our own washer and dryer. Our new apartment had a second bedroom we could take turns using as an office, a bathroom with a shower not requiring an arcane contraption bolted to a turn-of-the-previous-century faucet, electricity modern enough to accommodate a hair dryer, central air and heat, two stories, a kitchen the size of our former bedroom. A dishwasher would give me more time to try new recipes. When the property manager described the complex as a quiet community, we had no reason not to believe her.

A video store sat on the edge of the complex, one more place we wouldn't have to drive to. Our first night in the new apartment we rented *Office Space*, which neither of us had seen. Because Meredith grew frustrated when we browsed, I tried to come with titles in mind. The film's beleaguered hero had just been asked to come in on a Saturday when our walls and floor began to quake.

We went next door and introduced ourselves, trying to be friendly about our request to turn down the music. A trio of undergrads, the neighbors were polite enough, if unapologetic. After the third night in a row, we escalated our complaint to the property manager.

Some couples, when confronted with an external conflict, cultivate an us-against-the-world mentality that strengthens their bond. This did not happen with us. The cold war with the neighbors extended to other units in the complex. After cops broke up a parking lot concert, complete with a stage and squealing girls, an angry, anonymous note on our mailbox blamed us for calling the police. Perhaps our next-door neighbors fingered us as haters of noise.

On top of this, recent pain in Meredith's hands and arms kept getting worse. Often they were numb by the end of the day. When anti-inflammatories didn't relieve the pain, surgery looked more and more likely.

Around this time, the editor of a small literary journal in Texas called to accept one of my short stories. The payment of contributor copies and a one-year subscription wouldn't pay any bills, but news that my work was finally going to be published was welcome encouragement when I was struggling to feel like a writer.

Poetry and fiction were different forms, so it made sense, I convinced myself, for Meredith and me not to show each other our work. But it hadn't always been this way. In the early days, before we were more than friends, I had given her my short stories to read and she had given me a stack of her poems. I had been relieved when she said nice things about my work, even more relieved when her poems were good. Two years into our fraying relationship, she had stopped writing and I didn't dare show her what I was working on, wary of adding one more item to a lengthening list of my inadequacies.

Sometimes I still believed in my writing, believed it could save us. Publishing a book could mean a tenure-track job, benefits, a home without cardboard-thin walls shared with neighbors now leaving beer bottles and cigarette butts on our doorstep in protest against our noise complaints. Meredith wouldn't have to work an ostensible data-entry job that was the cause of what her doctor had diagnosed as carpal tunnel syndrome. She could start writing again.

We didn't go out much. In our social life, I tended to defer to Meredith, as I did with our diet, what we watched on TV, how long we stayed at parties. I treated her happiness as an equation, hoping these concessions would offset everything I couldn't do. Never was this feeling more pronounced than the days following her carpal tunnel surgery, after which she wasn't allowed to drive or lift anything heavier than a mug.

We were on our way to a follow-up with the hand specialist when it sounded like our car ran over something. Meredith had been cleared to drive if I shifted gears for her. We pulled onto a side street, and I put the car in park. As soon as we got out, we saw, which is to say Meredith saw, all four of our tires were flat.

We knew right away what had happened. A month earlier, we had exited our apartment to find two flat tires, the black plastic caps missing from their stems. You can place a hairpin in the nozzle and let out the air without actually damaging the tire, explained the female police officer, who recommended not filling out a report since our property had not actually been damaged. At least we were prepared this time, a recently purchased air compressor in the trunk of our car.

What were we going to do? What *could* we do? If my response to the first flattening of our tires was any indication, absolutely nothing. The closest thing to a fight I had ever gotten into was swinging my backpack at a fellow seventh grader, who responded in kind before the vice principal intervened. If my eyesight were better, would I be brave enough to knock on the neighbors' door? Throw a punch? We weren't even sure which neighbors were the culprits.

Soon enough they would no longer be our problem. After the first incident, we began the search for a new apartment. Our legally binding signatures on another lease seemed the only assurance that Meredith and I were going to be together in a few months. I had long blamed myself for the frustration of errands, but Meredith's conversation with a friend at a recent party confirmed I wasn't the only one who blamed me. Under what she must have thought the cover of loud music, she told a former classmate that she wasn't sure if she and I were going to make it. Being with me, she added in not-so-hushed tones, was "just so overwhelming."

The times she didn't regard me as invisible, I was a mistake for which she felt the need to apologize. Embarrassed as I always was for not seeing someone waving to me, a DO NOT ENTER sign, a credit card being handed back to me, Meredith seemed more embarrassed than I was.

Never was I more mortified or Meredith more sheepish when she was apologizing for my blunders than at her sister's wedding, where I met her family for the first time. Not having paid close enough attention to the movement of people in the small circle where we stood, I confused Meredith's mother with her great-aunt.

During an argument, Meredith confessed she hated going to parties with me. She felt an obligation, she said, to constantly check on me, make sure I was doing okay.

"You could always not check on me," I said.

"It just seems like you're never having a good time."

If I seemed unhappy at parties, it was because the only parties we attended were at the houses of her friends, and seeing Meredith having fun, the fun she rarely had when we were alone, was never reassuring. One Saturday night she had fallen asleep while watching movies at her best friend's house. In a panicked insomnia, unable to reach either of them by phone, I feared she had left me. The original sin of how we had gotten together kept my fear of her infidelity at a low simmer. I had no reason to distrust her, but if she was happier with her friends, why wouldn't she be happier with someone other than me?

"I feel like your caretaker," she said. "I'm sorry, but I do."

Crushing as this was to hear, it made little sense. How could *she* be *my* caretaker when, since she'd developed carpal tunnel, I had done one hundred percent of the cooking and cleaning? And if I was no chef or professional housekeeper, I had gotten better at both.

I massaged Meredith's forearms and hands, rubbed vitamin E into the scar from the surgery for fifteen minutes four times a day. Doing this in the morning meant waking extra early before the 8:00 classes I had been assigned five days a week. Meredith struggled mightily not to conflate her resentment of the predawn hour with resentment of me.

We still loved each other. We said so frequently. We continued to make love, if not as often as we used to, but wasn't that normal for a couple who's been together more than two years? When Meredith told me how attractive I was, her

words retained a sense of wonder. That this was the only compliment I ever received, along with praise for my cooking and
command of pop culture trivia, filled me with the opposite
of self-confidence. Nor did my self-image benefit from how
many of her Christmas and birthday gifts were suggestions
for improvement: button-down shirts, which I rarely wore;
low-rise, boot-cut jeans that hugged my backside more thoroughly than the relaxed fit I probably should have abandoned
in the early nineties; hair product that dried with a more natural sheen than the hair gel I probably should have abandoned
in the mid-nineties. Other gifts included a *Queer Eye for the
Straight Guy* wall calendar, *The Everything Slow Cooker Cookbook*,
stainless steel measuring cups, a bamboo cutting board, and
other kitchen gadgets. They weren't bad gifts, only gifts she
wanted me to have more than I wanted to have them. And if
they made me easier to love, more indispensable, I was grateful for every one of them.

Carpal tunnel surgery was and was not a success. The tiny cut
performed with a laser alleviated most of the pain in her right
wrist, but now she was suffering as much pain and numbness
in her left wrist, on which the doctor hadn't thought it necessary to operate. More troubling, by the time she returned to
work after two months of short-term disability, she had developed soreness in her knees. This soreness spread to her ankles,
even her toes. One day I was peeling garlic in the kitchen when
she came home from work. I called out to her. Minutes went
by with no response.

I found her seated at the top of the stairs. "Are you okay?"

She stared at the far wall. "It took me five minutes to climb ten steps," she said.

I helped her to her feet. I hugged her, waiting for her to cry, but she was too stunned for tears.

Some days were better than others. The morning of her appointment with an orthopedic specialist was one of the better days. Skeptically, reluctantly, the doctor referred her to a rheumatologist. The new specialist listened as Meredith described her symptoms. I offered elaboration, some details she forgot. The doctor ran tests. I helped Meredith down from the examining table. For once, we felt like a team, never more so than when tests showed nothing definitive and the doctor implied Meredith's symptoms might be psychological.

"I'm in pain," she told him, her voice unsteady.

The doctor said he believed her. "Your pain can be legitimate even if there is no physiological cause."

Many graduates of our MFA program received one-year contracts to teach full time at the university, but I was only offered two sections of composition on an adjunct basis. When the opportunity arose for additional classes at another school across town, I jumped at the chance. Minutes after accepting the position, I wondered how the hell I would get across town three days a week.

Greensboro's bus routes on the city's website, depicted with pictures rather than words, were inscrutable to my screen reader. When I called to ask which bus would take me from point A to point B, I got a referral to the same website that had prompted me to pick up the phone.

"My eyes are bad. I'm having trouble reading the maps." It was always easier to admit this over the phone.

The woman on the line gave me the bus number I would catch on the edge of one campus, which would take me to the downtown depot, where another bus would take me to the campus of my second employer. The total commute time, if all buses were punctual, would be one hour fourteen minutes. The distance? Two miles.

A week before the new semester, Meredith took me to the bus station so I could gather more info. My concerns were many, not least how I'd know I was getting on the correct bus. Would I have to ask which bus this was every time I climbed aboard? While I'd be waiting at bus stops outside the depot, how many buses might try to pick me up before the right one came along? As soon as we stepped inside the station, another question presented itself: Which of these half dozen windows was the one I needed? Meredith, as usual, stood two feet behind me, refusing to lead the way. Her outgoing personality before we began dating seemed as much a cultivated façade as my own efforts to pass for a sighted man.

I could tell which windows had lights on and which ones didn't. Beyond that, I had no idea which lighted windows were manned, which lighted windows were designated for buses and which ones were for trains. I could have asked Meredith these questions, but it also seemed Meredith could tell me without my having to ask. Her scarcely suppressed annoyance every time I needed her to read me cooking directions printed on a freezer bag in small white letters, fill out tax forms, or make a selection on a DVD's menu screen never made me glad

I had asked for her help. Thus, I stepped to the first window and hoped for the best.

"Honey, you need that window," said the woman.

"Which window?" I figured she was pointing, but hoped she would clarify with words.

"That one right there."

I thanked her, hoping Meredith had been paying attention.

"Why don't you just tell people you can't see?" Meredith would ask. It was a fair question. It also wasn't one she asked on this day. Three more years would pass before she asked it because, unbeknownst to me, the same eggshells on which I walked, trying so diligently not to ask her for help, lay beneath her feet as she dutifully avoided mentioning my blindness.

I stepped away from the window. Meredith said nothing. Did she *want* me to ask her for help? Was she waiting for me to say it in as many words? Sometimes it felt as though she were eager for me to make a mistake, to teach me a lesson, to demonstrate her superiority.

I approached another window. "Is this where I would transfer buses?"

"Yes, sir. Right out that door."

Again with the pointing. Again with the demonstrative adjective. I thanked him and stepped away from the window. I tried to swallow the lump in my throat. I tried again. The lump grew.

I turned to Meredith with what must have been red-rimmed eyes. "Why won't you ever help me?"

"What?"

I turned away from her.

TOO LONG TO STOP NOW   155

"What do you want me to do?"

I made my way to the farthest wall. Webs of dark lines in a large frame might have been a map. To my eyes, it was a windshield riddled with bullets. For several minutes I stood there, pretending to chart a route to anywhere I wanted to go. To anyone in the depot, I was the ordinary commuter I pretended to be, and this is why keeping my secret felt so important, so necessary, so good.

"What do you want me to do?" Meredith asked over my shoulder. Her voice had softened, but her tone had not.

I mumbled a response.

"What?"

"I said I'll fucking walk to work."

Our first session of couples counseling got off to an inauspicious start. Meredith's anxiety about finding an unfamiliar address made us half an hour early, and we sat silently in the dark car until it was time for our evening appointment. Our counselor, a warm, serious woman who reminded me of the nicer of two lunch ladies from elementary school, practiced out of her home, a ritzy, three-story Victorian in the far-out suburbs. Our counselor had glasses of ice water poured for us on a glass coffee table. The sound of the former crashing onto the latter alerted me to their presence.

"I'm sorry. I didn't . . ." I trailed off.

Our counselor deduced what had happened. In a preliminary phone conversation, Meredith had debriefed her on the nature of our problems, which is to say my blindness.

I watched in shame while our counselor cleaned up the mess.

The glass had not broken. Even if it had, she assured me they weren't expensive. My bigger concern was what this accident said about our hopes of treating our relationship's worsening symptoms. I and my eyes were the ones on trial here, and any efforts on my part to downplay the impact of my disability on everyday life had been undermined by this inadvertent confession.

The counselor asked how Meredith and I had met, what we liked about each other, what we hoped to gain from counseling. Perhaps because I was the underdog, I got to go first.

"I'd like us not to be angry at each other all the time," I said in response to the latter question.

"So you would like to repair this relationship?" she said.

"Yes."

The counselor asked Meredith the same question.

After some consideration, she said, "I want to know if it can be repaired."

Her answer didn't fill me with optimism. I wanted strategies for how we might modify our dynamic, cope with the less compatible elements of our personalities. It seemed she wanted a claims adjustor to declare our banged-up relationship totaled beyond repair.

Soon enough, in what our counselor might have thought a subtler transition than it seemed to me, the subject shifted to my eyes. Less expected were the tears that accompanied the rote details of my vision loss. To my further surprise, before we had mined the depths of my condition, the counselor shifted the focus away from me.

"Now, Meredith, why don't you tell me about your recent health problems."

Meredith described her carpal tunnel surgery and the joint pain she was now experiencing. The newest symptoms included a morning facial rash and an expanding bald spot on her scalp. The apocalyptic search results of googling medical symptoms is a trite punch line, but when doctors have dismissed you as at best overstressed and at worst mentally troubled, WebMD seems better than nothing. Possible diagnoses ranged from the ever-popular cancer to rheumatoid arthritis, all of them listing some telltale symptom Meredith did not possess. The terror of not knowing what's wrong can be overwhelming, but knowing what you have is only preferable if what you have is treatable.

By the time Meredith brought our counselor up to speed, our first session was tied: tears to tears.

Despite encouraging feedback from friends and professors who had read my finished novel, revisions were hard to fit into a schedule with four classes and three different syllabi on two campuses, every weekday beginning with a 6:00 a.m. alarm. Whenever I had time to revise, I didn't have the energy, and vice versa. It felt like a small miracle when I printed a new draft of the manuscript and mailed it to the literary agent of a friend who had read the most recent version. The chances of a positive response were one in a million, probably less when I discovered, weeks after my trip to the post office, an egregious typo on page one, but it was a relief to put my faith in something other than love.

By my estimate, I was walking more than forty miles a week. The first day I hoofed it from one campus to the other, I came home with burning toes and crackling arches, ascending the stairs with a limp I failed to conceal from Meredith. The next weekend, she insisted on taking me shopping for more supportive footwear.

Sore feet weren't the only complication from my long commute. I didn't mention to Meredith the spills I had taken on compacted bridge ice, or the inaugural walk in which I overshot the campus entrance by several blocks, or the direction of traffic on one street I must have mistaken because I was five or ten feet from the sidewalk when a horn sounded, sending me into a sprint and a long, accidentally balletic broad jump onto the curb. When I reached the sidewalk, two young men on bicycles greeted me in a friendly tone that suggested we had met before. They wore matching overcoats and white shirts. I made small talk, trying to place their voices, trying to forget that I might have been the victim of vehicular manslaughter.

"You guys get moved in all right?" one of them asked.

"We did," I said, realizing these were the Mormon missionaries who had been passing by our new apartment while we were unloading the U-Haul.

Being the one lifting most of the furniture, I happily accepted their offer to help. Less enthusiastic about their arrival, Meredith pulled me aside while the missionaries wrestled with one of our dressers, whispering in my ear who and what they were. Since she'd left the church during college, the presence of Mormons had made her anxious, fearful they might drag her to a Mormon gulag. I shrugged, finding my lower back more bothersome than their charity. To Meredith's silent horror, my mom, who had driven from West Virginia to help us move, invited the Mormons out to lunch after we had unloaded the truck, her treat.

I shook the Mormons' hands, thanking them again for their help. They got back on their bikes and pedaled down the sidewalk. What were the odds, in a city of three hundred thousand, of running into them again, right here, right now? In a good novel, every action, every line of dialogue, every description is there for a reason. If life were a novel, it could use a good editor—the pacing is way off, for one thing—but it's impossible not to search for meaning in certain coincidences.

The parallel between Meredith's debilitating illness and my own disability seemed so obvious, so ham-handed, a writer could never get away with it. This twist in our relationship, this reversal of our former roles as caretaker and charge, could be an opportunity for new empathy. Our counselor seemed to be leading us down this path before asking Meredith, at the end of our third session, if the two of them could meet one on one. Less subtly than our counselor, while massaging vitamin E into Meredith's arms before bed when I wanted nothing more than to close my eyes and fall into a deep sleep, I told her it might be a good thing if she could finally understand what it felt like to need help for simple things. Maybe she could develop some patience when it came to the supermarket, another passive-aggressive extravaganza from which we had just returned.

"It doesn't work like that," she said.

"Why not?"

"What if I keep getting worse? What if it gets to where neither of us can drive?"

So much for empathy. Hers or mine.

Meredith went to two solo counseling sessions before telling me she didn't want to go anymore. "I don't feel like I'm getting anything out of it," she said.

I didn't ask her to elaborate, didn't try to change her mind. What could I say? What else could I do but massage her forearms, her hands, hoping for the electricity she once felt?

The call came on a summer afternoon.

"Is this J.T.?" said the older man on the line.

"It is."

"I wasn't sure if you went by James or J.T. Writers and these initials," he said, and laughed warmly. Then he told me his name.

I had met Bill at a dinner party the second year in the MFA program. His wife was a visiting author, and his stepson a member of the faculty.

"Well, I've read your novel," said the literary agent to whom I had mailed it months earlier. He had a gentle, patrician voice.

I braced myself for the letdown. I could already tell this was a courtesy call.

"I thought it was hilarious and quite charming," he said.

But . . . but . . . but . . .

"I'd be glad to send it out for you when the time comes."

The time. What time? Send it out?

He explained concerns he had about the plot, the latter third of the book in particular, and asked if I'd be willing to take another stab at it. I tried to suppress the dozen exclamation points after my affirmative response. We agreed to talk again soon, and when he called me "old chap" I felt a firm handshake welcoming me through the wrought-iron gates of American letters.

"Oh my God," Meredith stage-whispered into her work phone. "That's amazing."

She wanted to take me out for a celebratory dinner, but I thought we should hold off until the novel actually sold. We settled on cheesecake from our favorite bakery.

We had been doing much better in recent months—the last year, really—our frustrations with each other increasingly rare. Somehow we had fallen into a rhythm that seemed to work, an intricate tango of moods and patience that allowed for regular pockets of joy. Precisely how we had managed this I wasn't sure. It helped that she was no longer in physical pain.

After seeing the doctor who implied her symptoms were in her head, Meredith pleaded with her primary care physician for a referral to a different rheumatologist. This one, a woman, believed right away that she was sick. While not necessarily lupus, Meredith's symptoms struck the new rheumatologist as consistent with an autoimmune disorder. She prescribed medication that began to relieve her joint pain in a matter of days. Within a few weeks, she felt better than she had felt before the first inklings of pain in her wrist. In a couple of months, all her hair had grown back, and the rashes on her face had gone away.

I worked mornings and afternoons rewriting my novel. In the evenings, Meredith used our computer to research places to live in Pittsburgh. She had been offered admission and scholarships to a master's program in library science, a field

she had been considering for a couple of years. Grateful that
we had landed on a sturdy plateau of contentment, I was glad
to move wherever she got in. It would only be for two years.

Week after week, new and strange complications arose
with Meredith's graduate program. Most troubling was the
school's tendency to lose any record of their offer of a scholarship. Next they lost her letter accepting the scholarship.
The next thing you know, we joked, they'll lose her offer of
admission, which, right on cue, happened a few weeks later.
Each time, after multiple phone calls and apologies from the
program, someone eventually located some kind of confirma-
tion of Meredith's existence, but when it happened again, this
time while we were in Pittsburgh looking for an apartment,
it felt like a sign we'd be foolish to ignore. Just as dispiriting
were the apartments we toured, most of them third floors
of family homes or one-bedroom units with bars in the windows. After a long talk, we canceled my appointments with
composition chairs at two colleges and hit the road back to
North Carolina.

By now, Meredith was having second thoughts about
library science. When she found an editing program in Seattle
that offered a certificate rather than a degree, I didn't know
how to tell her it sounded like a bad idea. It was possible I
didn't want her to move across the country. With the program
starting in November and my academic year already under-
way, both of us moving made no sense.

Dates and miles weren't the only numbers to consider. The
costs of an apartment in Seattle, our apartment in Greensboro, Meredith's tuition and books, both our student loans,

her dwindling savings and lack of a job once she moved there, and our combined monthly income of eighteen hundred dollars once Meredith quit her job seemed like variables in an unworkable equation.

But if I had learned anything in this year we had been on solid ground, happy even, it was how much Meredith's countenance improved whenever I agreed with her. It was only for seven months, and if finances were a concern, they concerned me much less when Bill phoned in October to say the novel was ready to send to publishers.

I googled how long it took an agent to sell a novel, average advances for a debut novel, recent deals brokered by my agent, novels edited by the first editor to whom we sent the manuscript, film rights for novels, whether publishers read manuscripts during holidays. When the highs and lows produced by these results became too great, I entered other search terms: platinum vs. white gold, conflict-free diamond, color vs. clarity, princess cut vs. emerald cut.

We missed each other deeply. Meredith said so tearfully in all our phone calls. It wasn't simply loneliness. Two of her closest friends lived in Seattle. I still had my life in Greensboro. Taking the next step didn't feel like a decision as much as gravity. I hoped to hear an editor say yes before asking Meredith to marry me, but as weeks became months I decided one question shouldn't depend on the answer to the other.

"Yes," she said. "Of course."

Meredith had returned to North Carolina for Christmas, and we had never been happier to see each other. Separated by the width of a continent, we'd forgotten every source of tension, our empty apartments amplifying everything worth missing.

Our money was running out fast, and Meredith's editing program seemed less and less like a career path. With nibbles from editing jobs back in North Carolina, she dropped out between quarters and came back to plan our wedding.

One day in early May I came home to a message from my agent on the answering machine. Bill said my full name in a jovial manner that seemed to imply good news. "Give me a call," he said.

I paced the apartment as I dialed, trying to decide which room to be in when my life changed. Meredith had gone out to run an errand. Bill's assistant put him on the line, and I imagined the moment my fiancée got home: me lifting her off the floor, spinning her around as I had when her first poems were accepted. You will not be marrying a failure, I thought.

Bill asked if I had taken a look at the rejections his assistant had scanned and emailed me the week before. Half a dozen letters on publishing house letterhead gave brief, polite explanations why they would not be purchasing my novel. One editor said she had bought too many novels similar to mine. Another explained he couldn't buy a wrestling novel because women wouldn't be interested in wrestling and men didn't buy books.

"What do you make of them?" Bill asked.

I didn't know. None of the editors offered ideas for revision. I asked Bill what he made of them.

"I'm afraid," he began, "that we might have gotten everything we're going to get out of submitting this particular novel."

I sat down in my desk chair. Meredith's car door closed in the driveway.

We married at a bed-and-breakfast outside Asheville, North Carolina, not quite halfway between our respective homes. A terrific editing job had taken Meredith to Nashville over the summer, and in a few months, at the end of the fall semester, I would join her. That the bride handled most of the planning didn't strike me as unusual. Meredith, who rarely listened to music, asked me to pick the song for our first dance. Most decisions were simplified by budgetary concerns— somehow, with fewer than fifty guests, the price tag quickly ballooned to ten thousand dollars, then twelve, finally settling around fifteen.

We held hands while repeating *I will*. The pastor father of Meredith's college roommate officiated. We had constructed our vows from examples we read online, editing out references to religion and wifely servitude. Meredith's older sister, a classical pianist, played the processional. The rest of her family occupied two full rows, their attendance our wedding gift.

"The one thing we didn't need," Meredith joked.

I smiled, trying to catch Meredith's eye. She faced me, seemed to return my smile. I could hear Mom crying in the front row. Dad sat a few rows behind her, the two of them having divorced during my final year of grad school. They had met in their late teens and married after a few months of dating. Over the years they had become different people. Meredith and I had met in our mid-twenties and dated for five

years. At twenty-nine, how far could we be from our permanent selves?

"The maps they gave us were out of date by years," began
the Adrienne Rich poem Meredith had one of her friends read
during the ceremony.

Halfway through our vows, I thought I was on the verge of
tears, but the urge went away. Later, Meredith would thank
me for not crying, which would have made her cry, which
would have ruined her makeup for the photo shoot following
our nuptials.

Meredith rejected my initial choices for our first-dance
song for being too long. She didn't like the thought of people
staring at us on the dance floor more than was absolutely necessary. None of the songs we had listened to while falling in
love sounded quite right. In the end, I went with Otis Red-
ding's "I've Been Loving You Too Long to Stop Now," a song I
didn't think we had ever heard in each other's presence. I first
encountered it in a third-season episode of the show *Nip/Tuck*,
after one of the plastic surgeons is left at the altar. We took
our places on the dance floor. Friends and family cheered us
on until the three-minute song faded well short of the part
where Otis begs to "please don't make me stop now."

Without the funds for another trip, our honeymoon was two
additional nights at the bed-and-breakfast. Instead of festivities
leading up to the wedding, Meredith asked guests to hang out
with us afterward. At times it felt more like her college reunion.
Counting spouses and significant others, a dozen of her friends
stayed on. Of the people I had invited, only Ron and his wife
and Jenny and her boyfriend remained in town. Rizwan, who

was completing his medical residency in New York, had driven all night to make the ceremony, napping at a rest area. On call the next day, he had to leave after the reception.

During meals in Asheville, Meredith sat with her friends and I sat with mine. This made sense: these were people we didn't see that often, and Meredith and I had the rest of our lives together.

The evening after the wedding, we migrated to the recreation room of the bed-and-breakfast, where Meredith's friends hooked their cameras up to the big-screen TV for a wedding slide show. In the back corner, Ron and I idly slid billiard balls across the pool table.

"This is like one of those nostalgic VH1 shows," he said, referencing the ubiquitous retrospectives of the day—*I Love the 70s, I Love the 80s, I Love the 90s.*

"I Love Yesterday," I agreed.

8
THE DEFINITION
OF FAITH

FOR MORE THAN A month after I moved to Nashville, Meredith and I spoke only perfunctorily. Neither of us mentioned the Saturday night phone call from early November. If I didn't bring it up, I could almost convince myself it never happened.

I can't believe we got married, she said. We never fixed anything, she said. I will not be complicit in your lie, she said, but her words had acquired the hazy, illogical feel of a nightmare. Should I move to Nashville? I remembered saying, and whatever her answer had been, here I was.

Citing wedding debts and my planned unemployment during the spring semester, we didn't exchange Christmas presents. More than a lack of money, it seemed a tacit admission that neither of us knew what the other wanted. As my thir-tieth birthday approached, Meredith simply asked what she could get me, and I gave her the names of a couple of CDs. My thirtieth-birthday dinner was an overcooked calzone from a takeout pizzeria a mile from our apartment, which I selected so Meredith wouldn't get lost in this city that remained unfa-miliar after more than six months.

Those weighty conversations from early November hung like dialogue balloons over our heads. We had yet to revisit anything we said. Our reticence reminded me of lines from a poem I heard someone read aloud in graduate school: It isn't the dirt that weakens our clothes, but the constant washing.

At the time of my first novel's death, I had written fewer than twenty new pages, best characterized as a *project* rather than a novel. I was twenty-nine years old, hardly ancient, but I had been writing fiction since I was sixteen. Thirteen years is either a lot of time to throw away to pursue a new career, or a lot of time to be doing something and not yet know what you're doing.

I was haunted by the voice of an award-winning writer in graduate school who described one of my short stories as *ami-able.* "I'd borrow tools from it," he said, "but I wouldn't buy it a beer."

What else was I qualified to do? What else might I enjoy doing one-tenth as much as writing? These might have been questions to explore with my then fiancée, a fellow writer, but even in the halcyon days of our most peaceful coexistence, we rarely spoke about writing, let alone our personal failures.

When Meredith finally read my novel—I had asked her to proofread the final revision before sending it to Bill—it was the first time she had read my work since we were graduate students. She liked it, thought it was good, was convinced it would sell, but her compliments could have been influenced by the praise of a respected literary agent. Bill's endorsement, I knew, had given me the courage to let her read it.

In the week following my novel's failure, Meredith and I might have bonded over the fragile emotions that make a creative life so difficult. Instead, we turned on the television, landing on a rerun of *Inside the Actors Studio*, Dustin Hoffman being fawned over by James Lipton. The two-time Academy Award winner, who had kept me company throughout college on my *Rain Man* poster, described the early days of his acting career, watching peers find success in film roles while he waited for his big break. He continued to perform at the Pasadena Playhouse, and it was there, he said, that he realized if this was all the success he ever achieved, he would still be happy. He loved acting; it didn't matter where he did it.

The next morning I opened the file containing the first pages of what might or might not be a novel. I read the first paragraph and deleted it. I read the second paragraph and deleted it. I found a few sentences I liked enough not to delete and started writing.

"Are we ever going to talk about . . ." Meredith finally said one night before bed. Her serious tone made it easy to finish her thought.

"What is there to talk about?" I said.

"Everything," Meredith said after a protracted pause.

She said I had not attempted to make a life for myself in Nashville, and she wasn't wrong. Because I had supported us while she took editing classes in Seattle, my wife was giving me the spring semester to finish my new novel. It was my best chance at a job more gainful than adjuncting, which paid even less in Tennessee than in North Carolina. Why shouldn't I put all my energy into writing?

On top of that, there was next to nothing within walking distance of our apartment complex. The sidewalk in front of it ended in a strip mall on one side and a residential road on the other. Besides retrieving our mail from the bank of metal boxes and working out in our complex's tiny fitness center, I left the apartment only to run the weekly grocery gauntlet with Meredith. Where else was there to go?

"You haven't made any effort to take the bus," she said.

"Where am I supposed to take it?"

"You could meet me at my office. We could do something after work."

"Do what exactly?"

My wife stared at the muted TV. When we met, Meredith didn't have a working television. Now she planned her evenings around more than half a dozen shows, diligently programming the VCR whenever she wasn't going to be home. We had an office, but I had ceded it to Meredith, situating my desktop in the living room, adjacent to the TV stand. Whenever one of her shows came on that I wasn't interested in, which was most of them, I used the evening to work on the novel. From time to time, Meredith offered to move to the bedroom, where we had a second TV, but I always refused the offer. Writing while Meredith was in the room, while she was watching *House Hunters* or *What Not to Wear*, made me feel like I was doing something, getting somewhere, when most of the time I felt nothing but trapped.

Checking out books on tape was next to impossible in Tennessee. The state library for the blind and physically handicapped, understaffed and underfunded, rarely had my selections, although they were listed as available in the online catalog. Often they forwarded my requests to neighboring states. Books took months to arrive, when they arrived at all.

I was more isolated in Nashville than I had been in Morgantown without friends. At least here I could blame my loneliness on someone other than myself. Whenever I asked Meredith for help finding the closest hair salon, or if the traffic light near our apartment had a turn signal, she became so frustrated we fell into a tense silence lasting several hours.

"Have you ever considered getting a cane?" she asked me when I expressed safety concerns about crossing the highway to the closest bus stop.

I laughed at the suggestion. "What would that do?"

"For one thing, it would let drivers know you have trouble seeing. They would be more careful when you're crossing a street."

"As opposed to the fully sighted people crossing streets they just plow into?"

Meredith sighed. She didn't know how justifiable her safety concerns were. I had never told her—I had never told anyone—about the times I had almost been hit by a car. If

I had, I might have heard worry in my wife's voice rather than scorn.

"Why is it so important to you that I announce to people what I can't see?"

"Why is it so important to you that people don't know?"

"Maybe because every time I acknowledge to you what I can't see or do, your reaction is exhaustion. Every time I make a mistake, you apologize for me like I'm a dog who wet the floor."

I wasn't the only one who made mistakes. The day before our wedding, applying for our license in the Asheville court-house, I had nothing in my wallet showing my Social Security number. A last-minute fax of a life insurance policy saved the day, but this would be the plot of our how-we-almost-couldn't-get-married story. Yet Meredith was the one who arrived at the courthouse seven minutes prior to closing time, having forgotten she would lose an hour in East Tennessee when the time zone changed.

Meredith's mistakes were the kind we forgot. Mine were incorrigible. I was incorrigible. And my inability to correct my mistakes, to become a man for whom his wife didn't apologize, made it hard to acknowledge what I *could* fix, or try to. It also made it hard to remember why we had gotten married.

Meredith composed herself. "How would we go on a trip together? To another country?"

Her use of *would* rather than *will* hurt worse than the question.

"How would you read signs in an airport or a train station?"

"If you were with me, why wouldn't you read them?"

"I don't want to be the one who always has to do that. Constantly. For the rest of my life."

"You knew I couldn't read signs when we first got together."

Light from the TV flashed on the floor. It seemed so loud even with the sound off.

Meredith bowed her head. "Your world is so small," she said.

My world didn't feel small. To me, it was enormous, a gigantic mystery I would never solve.

"I'm never going to be able to read signs," I said. "If that's what you need me to do, that would probably fall into the category of an irreconcilable difference."

More silence, more tears. From both of us.

"Do you know that quotation from Chekhov?" Meredith asked.

"Probably not."

"He said, 'Any idiot can get through a crisis. It's the day-to-day living that wears you down.'"

"Is this the crisis or the day-to-day living?"

One morning after Meredith left for work, I got down one of my unpacked boxes from the shelf of my closet. At the bottom, beside extension cords and my old microcassette recorder, sat the small white box. Its contents remained sealed in plastic. The pills were bound in packets of ten, each sheet holding a dozen pills. I transferred a few sheets to my nightstand, tucking them beneath my dress socks and handkerchiefs, and returned the boxes to my closet.

A few times after my trip to Tokyo, the doctor we had seen sent us another year's supply of the experimental drug we had gone there to obtain, free of charge. Because the medicine had done nothing to improve my vision, I eventually stopped taking them. These particular pills might have been a decade old.

If faith is the dogged belief in that which cannot be known or seen, I wasn't sure how much faith I had in my marriage, my novel, or the God to whom I'd prayed when I was a child and to whom I found myself praying again as I poured a glass of water.

Praying itself is an act of faith, I read somewhere. So, too, is the act of writing, and falling asleep in the same bed with someone who doesn't seem to like you anymore, and swallowing two little pills that hadn't done what you hoped they would do when you'd first carried them to a water fountain in a Japanese hospital fourteen years ago.

It was a cool April morning when I finished the first draft of my new novel. I pressed CONTROL-HOME, moving the cursor to the top of the document, and inserted a blank page. I typed the title, *In Light of Recent Events*, and increased the font to a size befitting a book cover.

I phoned Meredith at work to tell her the news. In recent weeks, we had progressed from polite to friendly. I was cautiously optimistic about what lay on the other side of friendly. Her response was muted—perhaps mine should have been more reserved, first draft that it was—but I could hear she was trying. If we hadn't cured our unhappiness three years ago, we had at least gotten the symptoms under control. Why couldn't we do that again?

After hanging up, I checked the clock. I had twenty minutes until McDonald's stopped serving breakfast. For the most part, I had abandoned my life of fast food and Hot Pockets for single-origin coffees and homemade risotto, but nearby options were limited. Besides the Golden Arches, other shops and restaurants in the strip mall closest to our apartment, on our side of the busy four-lane, included a Rite Aid, TJ Maxx, Burger King, and a sub shop that called its sandwiches "grinders." Getting there required crossing an unlined two-lane road and multiple driveways, and traversing a narrow shoulder of the four-lane without a sidewalk. Sidewalks in our neighborhood—in all of Nashville, it seemed—were as common as palm trees.

Each time I reached the strip mall safely, I felt as though I had swum the English Channel. I never mentioned my furloughs from the apartment to Meredith. Telling her would imply it was noteworthy, and I didn't want her to think she was married to a man for whom a two-thousand-foot walk to get a Quarter Pounder with Cheese was a gold-star day.

"I thought you were out of deodorant," Meredith called one evening from the bathroom.

I used a brand Target and Kroger no longer carried, but after kneeling for several minutes in the first aisle of Rite Aid, I discovered it had not been discontinued. I told her where I had gotten it, my nonchalance belying how thrilled I was that she had noticed. That? Oh, nothing. Just swam to the bottom of the ocean to retrieve a necklace worn by a passenger on the *Titanic*. No big deal.

From the din of voices inside McDonald's, I gathered the late-breakfast crowd consisted of retirees and parents of young children. I got the cashier I had gotten my previous visit, a younger woman who smiled when she spoke. Her friendliness made our brief exchanges feel like we had a rapport.

"Anything else for you?" She asked this with what seemed like a sly smile.

I aimed my gaze at the menus, stealing another glance at the cashier. The hair under her hat seemed sandy brown, her teeth a flash of white.

"I think that'll do it," I said.

She thanked me for my credit card. Did she remember me from prior visits? If I could see her face, would I be able to tell?

I ate my Egg McMuffin in the corner booth, rethinking my snobbish views of American cheese. Its saltiness contrasted well with the English muffin, the gooey texture holding the sandwich together. Grease from the hash browns settled warmly in my stomach, and for the first time I understood, completely and with every taste bud, why they call it comfort food.

It's a myth that the other senses of the blind are superior to those of the fully sighted. Without our eyes, we simply pay more attention to what we hear, smell, taste, and feel. The subtleties of Picasso's Blue Period would always elude my limited acuity, but maybe I could develop an ear for jazz. In college, I dreamed of naming the perfume a girl was wearing, like Al Pacino in *Scent of a Woman*, but the closest I ever came was recognizing a few shampoos. I had learned to cook chilaquiles and cassoulet, describe the dusty finish of a quality Malbec, find tasting notes of lavender and champagne in a cup of Ethiopia Yirgacheffe coffee. How else could I make my world a little bigger?

I thought about the woman behind the counter, wishing I were the kind of person who talked to strangers, who could make real eye contact, transform meaningful looks into meaningful conversations. I wished I were a man capable of leaving a bad relationship, but I barely found the courage to leave the apartment. Watching something slip away bit by bit, on the other hand, growing accustomed to what is no longer there? This I did with expertise.

"Are you having a good day?" asked the possibly attractive woman. She was wiping down the adjacent table.

"I am," I said. "What about you?"

"It's a day," she said cheerfully.

I tried to think of something else to say, some kind of ice-breaker, a question, a joke.

She wiped down the swivel chairs fastened to the floor. I thought of a funny line, but now she was on the other side of the restaurant.

It seemed early to hear a key in the front door. Usually Meredith called if she was coming home early. I said hello from my computer. If she returned my greeting, it was too quiet for me to hear. My former employer in North Carolina had hired me to teach the first online version of the writing course I had taught in the classroom. I was typing an email to the colleague who had designed it. This would extend my daily confinement to the apartment for another semester or two, but the money was better than any college in Nashville might have paid me. Today was the first day of classes and the course's contents were still nowhere to be found. Between our dial-up Internet and the nervous, flaky colleague who wouldn't tell me if a syllabus for the course even existed, it had been a frustrating week.

I noticed Meredith standing behind me and got up from the computer. "What's wrong?"

She tried unsuccessfully to speak.

"Are you okay?"

"I, I, I . . ." The words came out slowly, her chest seeming to convulse. "I want, want, want."

They weren't words as much as connected syllables.

"Wa-wa-wa-wa-want." She managed a tiny breath. "Duh-duh-duh . . ."

She couldn't get it out, so I said it for her. "Divorce?"

"Ye-ye-ye-ye-ye-yes."

She continued to shake, to hyperventilate. I touched her arm. My wife flinched as though I had struck her. I waited for her to continue, waited for an explanation, waited for what I had been waiting for since last November.

No matter how prepared we are for an impact, how thoroughly we've braced ourselves, there's no such thing as a pain-free fall. There's a reason we still cry at funerals when loved ones die after a long illness. And sob we did while I made arrangements to return to Greensboro. Meredith's longest, deepest jag came while she was divvying up our receipts and warranties in her meticulous files of everything we had ever purchased. Mine came while I was washing dishes after the last meal I cooked for us, noticing a deep scratch in the expensive pan that had been a wedding gift.

A few days before leaving Nashville, I printed all 368 pages of the only thing I had to show for my time in Tennessee. In a couple of years, this tale of child stars trying to atone for bad decisions in their youth would become my second failed novel. On this day, however, every sheet falling into the tray of my printer was 8.5 by 11 inches of hope.

"What are you doing?" Meredith asked, laughing for the first time in I wasn't sure how long.

I let myself smile. I had stacked the pages of my novel on the linoleum by the front door and stepped on them with both feet. One of my favorite authors, Ann Patchett, described doing this with her first novel, seeing how much taller it made her. The manuscript I was certain would be my first book added three inches to my height, but for a few moments my head seemed to touch the ceiling.

9

THE D-WORD

IT HAD BEEN FIFTEEN years since I last visited an eye doctor. There was nothing they could tell me about my eyes that I didn't know. I had no reason to be nervous, I kept reminding myself.

Tentative voices filled the crowded waiting room, people bracing for bad news. They sounded older than me, some of them elderly. The office was in a small, one-story building, rather than a medical complex. The friend who brought me noted a pair of pawnshops on the walk from the parking garage.

A woman called my name from an open doorway. She led me to a dim room with an examining chair. I sat in it while she asked questions about my vision, transcribing my answers. I tried not to look at her when I spoke. After a decade and a half, feigning eye contact was a hard habit to break. I was here to prove what I couldn't see, not what I could.

After teaching a full load of four courses in the fall, I learned my spring schedule had been reduced to a single section of composition. The department chair, a new hire, blamed the vagaries of a new curriculum, but the online catalog showed that adjuncts who had been there less time than me had been assigned three and four sections.

Making ends meet on an adjunct's salary was already difficult when I was teaching a full load. On top of living expenses, credit card debt from my wedding was still going strong well after the marriage it produced. A couple of my colleagues waited tables for extra income, but refilling water glasses wasn't a skill I could add to my LinkedIn profile. A well-meaning friend mentioned a local job-placement organization called Industries for the Blind. All their jobs, someone told me over the phone, involved making brooms.

Googling employment for the visually impaired, I discovered some statistics said that as few as thirty percent of the blind had jobs. Perhaps this was my destiny. On the other hand, I had accomplished less than many blind people who acknowledged their disability. There were blind doctors. There were blind lawyers. "You don't write because you want to say something. You write because you have something to say," said F. Scott Fitzgerald. Did I know the difference? After three master's degrees, my list of publications consisted of a short story and a book review, neither of which resulted in payment.

I thought back to the Social Security checks I had gotten when I was younger. I had been grateful to finally earn a living, however meager, to scrub the money trail leading to my disability. Maybe the monthly payments could resume now that I was underemployed and making so little.

I called the Social Security office, and the person who answered informed me that my monthly income, combined with a small savings account and a few savings bonds, disqualified me from receiving my old Supplemental Security Income checks. Student loans, credit card debt, and monthly expenses didn't factor into their calculations. The representative did say my work history made me eligible for disability if I still met the threshold for legal blindness. She took down my date and time preferences for an appointment with an ophthalmologist.

The nurse dilated my pupils and left the room. Through the wall, another patient raised her voice, seemed to argue. How many of us were here at the behest of Social Security? How many lied about what they couldn't see? How many lied for half their lives about what they could?

The doctor had on what looked like jeans. His curt hello when he entered the room seemed consistent with a man whose patients disputed what he wrote in their charts. He read my answers to the nurse's questions and peered into my dilated eyes.

As long as it had been since my eyes were examined, I couldn't recall if doctors could see evidence of my condition. Results of a long-ago blood test proved I had Leber's hereditary optic neuropathy, but proof of mutated genes was not proof of blindness.

The doctor held a magnifying glass in one hand and a light in the other. A voice in the hall caught his attention. Moments later, a second doctor, female with a young-sounding voice, peered through the magnifying glass at my optic nerves. Did she see how pale they were, yellow instead of pink? the first doctor asked. Indeed she did.

They took turns shining a light into my eyes. The first doctor, noticing my occupation on my chart, asked where I taught. He shook my hand on his way out, relieved that I was what I said I was. In hindsight, the relief might have been mine.

I had signed a lease for the apartment where my friend Matt lived during graduate school. Across the street sat my own apartment from that period. My slanted floors and clanging radiators screamed student housing. Lonely nights triggered flashbacks to parties spent flirting with the poet who would become my wife, who would not be my wife much longer.

The last time I lived alone I was still eating Campbell's Chunky Soup and frozen chimichangas. Now I made tuna steaks and stuffed portobellos. Thus far, cooking for myself was less rewarding than cooking for two. Nor was I a fan of my kitchen's gas stove with its visible flames. Cook times were different from those with the electric stoves I had always used. One evening the burners wouldn't even turn on.

"Is the pilot light on?" asked my landlord, a sweet, elderly man who did his own maintenance.

"How would I find out?" I had lived my thirty-one years without encountering a pilot light.

Mr. Sandler explained where to look. I checked but couldn't see if it was on or off.

"I'm the one with the bad eyes," I said.

He said he'd be over in a little while.

The pilot light had gone out. Mr. Sandler struck a match and lit it. He asked if I thought I could light it myself if it went out again.

"I think so," I lied.

Another time, in late fall, I had awoken to what sounded like a running shower. The living room was a white cloud. It didn't smell like smoke. I tracked the sound to the radiator by the windows. The furniture was wet with steam. I couldn't get close enough to turn the heat off. I thought I had shut it off a week ago.

Mr. Sandler arrived with a toolbox. There was still sleep in his voice. I apologized for calling so early on a Sunday. I apologized again, more profusely, when he found the cause of the problem. In trying to turn off the heat the week before, I had unscrewed a valve that regulated the steam.

"Take care," said Mr. Sandler, letting himself out. In his tone I heard, Maybe you shouldn't be living on your own.

A letter informed me I had been approved for disability. Checks would not begin, however, until five months from the date I applied. Even before this news, time had begun to feel like my sworn enemy.

Unable to sleep, I perused Netflix, deciding on an episode of *30 Rock*. Twenty-two minutes later, I watched another. Twenty-two minutes after that, I wondered how I had ever filled the hours of a day.

I dragged my box of VHS tapes into the living room. In high school, my best friend teased me for refusing to watch movies on the VCR when I was by myself. There was nothing lonelier, I argued, than popping a tape into the VCR, knowing I was the only viewer on earth pressing PLAY at that exact moment. Watching a movie on cable made me part of an audience, even if we would never meet. There was, it turned out, something lonelier than watching a movie by myself.

Tom Cruise movies made up a third of my collection. At age twelve, when selecting a favorite actor seemed important, I decided the star of *Top Gun* would be mine. We were watching *Rain Man* in an eighth-grade class called Current Events, for a unit on mental illness. I felt worldly for enjoying the most recent Oscar winner for Best Picture, but also cool because it starred Tom Cruise.

Tom Cruise was one of life's winners. His gleaming, eye-crinkling smile seemed to say, I know the secret to having fun. It said, Maybe you know something I don't know, but I don't give a shit because I know everything I need to know.

Hollywood's most bankable star for a decade and a half, Tom Cruise felt the need, the need for speed, and single-handedly saved America from those Soviet planes, or something— honestly I never understood what was going on in the second half of *Top Gun*. In *A Few Good Men*, Jack Nicholson told Tom Cruise he couldn't handle the truth, but Jack Nicholson was quite wrong. As the titular character of *Jerry Maguire*, he told a woman he barely knew that she completed him. They got married and lived happily ever after.

A few weeks after I moved into my apartment, Mom drove down to help me get settled. The last time I saw her I had just moved to Nashville. She got along well with her daughter-in-law, and breaking the news that we were divorcing wasn't easy. With her and Dad's divorce only a few years old, she asked if my marriage had failed because I came from a broken home.

I told her not to be ridiculous. "My home wasn't broken when I left it," I said.

Not knowing how long it would take to find an apartment, I had let Meredith keep most of the furniture, largely hand-me-down. Mom helped me buy a bed to replace the air mattress I had been sleeping on. I was lucky to have parents who could help me financially. Dad was sending money to cover utilities until I got back on my feet. Needing my parents' help, on the other hand, was the opposite of independence.

Mom and I found end tables and a dresser at Goodwill. Carrying them in, we removed the dresser's drawers to reduce its weight. It had been motel furniture, with holes on top where the television had been screwed down. The drawers didn't go in as easily as they came out. I asked Mom for help fitting them into the well-worn grooves.

"You should do it. In case you have to take them out later," she said.

"I can't see where the tracks are."

Mom tried to explain their shape and location, how many inches they were from the front of the opening.

"I know where they are," I said, my voice rising. "I can't see to get them in the grooves."

"We never showed you how to do things for yourself," she said, this thrift store dresser seemingly a metaphor for my failed marriage. Single herself after twenty-seven years, the recent owner of her own insurance agency, Mom was learning her own lessons about independence.

I struggled with the drawers for another ten minutes, finally shoving them in crooked. Mom fixed them a few hours later.

I never had felt like much of a teacher. Like many writers, I had ended up in the classroom through inertia and a lack of options. Teaching only one class made me feel even more like an impostor. Even worse, my lone section of composition met online, giving me fewer reasons to leave the apartment.

Most of my students, I learned, had taken the online section because it was the only one still available. Every few days a student would email to ask when the course began, unaware it was online. Where their schedules listed the building and room number, it read *TBA*.

Subtracting the students who never made contact with me, the students who never turned anything in, and the students who dropped the course, the enrollment of twenty-five became fewer than ten by midterm. Everything I enjoyed about teaching, the real-time learning and thinking on my feet, class discussions and the laughter of students, was reduced to grading and answering emails. Even this, with so few students, filled the tiniest slice of my week.

My elaborate methods of hiding my disability in class were no longer necessary. Teaching online, I didn't have to match voices to areas of the classroom to learn student names. Since my first semester as a TA, I had forbidden students from raising their hands, to better prepare them, I explained, for real-world interaction. Outside the classroom, nobody needs permission to talk.

"We're all adults," I said. "Feel free to speak whenever you have something to say."

I pushed *Rain Man*, the first movie I ever owned, into the VCR. It was a Christmas gift from my parents my senior year of high school. After losing my sight, I found myself returning to my favorite movies, the ones I had seen enough times that I could watch them without my eyes.

That spring, Mrs. Jones assigned our final project for senior English.

"Choose a song, a movie, a poem—anything at all," she said, "and explain how its structure supports its meaning."

Rain Man came immediately to mind. The movie's road trip is a journey of self-discovery for Tom Cruise's character, who transforms from a callous businessman into a willing caretaker of the autistic brother he never knew he had.

A heated negotiation in the film's first minutes establishes Cruise as the cocky upstart he has played in his other films. "The fucking EPA!" he shouts, and my dad, who reached for this expletive with some regularity, expressed misgivings about including this scene in my presentation.

I phoned Mrs. Jones at home. Mrs. Jones phoned Principal Lohan. Permission to show Tom Cruise saying *fuck* was not granted, and for reasons I didn't yet understand, my entire presentation seemed in jeopardy. I wanted to show Tom Cruise being Tom Cruise before Dustin Hoffman's idiot savant hijacks the whole movie.

Although Hoffman received his second Oscar for playing the autistic brother, Cruise's is the more dynamic performance. Hoffman's might be the title role, but Cruise drives the action, figuratively and literally, piloting their late father's Buick Roadmaster convertible from Cincinnati to Los Angeles. Hoffman swears he is an excellent driver, but admits he has only ever driven "slow on the driveway."

Every time Dustin Hoffman came on the screen, I worried what my classmates would think of me. Like Hoffman, I could no longer drive. If classmates hadn't noticed my absence from the parking lot, they must have wondered why I wasn't in class on test days, noticed my special notebook paper and the handwriting I struggled to read with a 22× magnifier when I reviewed my notes. Like Hoffman, I spent a lot of time staring at the floor.

Eager to leave my apartment, I looked forward to faculty meetings. When they were over, I walked the two and a half miles back to my apartment. A ride home from one of my colleagues would mean doing nothing for hours while they taught afternoon classes. Reading an audiobook was out of the question. My Walkman-sized book player had died after a dozen years of valiant service. I didn't own a laptop. A desktop computer was theoretically mine to use in the cubicle I shared with two other adjuncts, but my outdated screen-reading software wasn't compatible with newer versions of Windows.

Passed in 1990, the Americans with Disabilities Act states that employers must provide reasonable accommodations to workers with disabilities, including special equipment an employee needs to do his or her job. Receiving those accommodations can be more complicated than simply asking for them. *Reasonable* rarely means the same to employers as it does to employees.

In my MFA program, when I was the fiction editor of the literary journal, the program's director, aware of my blindness, asked what I'd need to read and edit submissions in the journal's office. He passed along my request for a scanner and a computer with 64 megabytes of RAM to the department chair. The chair balked. Until the department secretary found both in a vacated office, it seemed the editorship would go to someone else.

The scanner the secretary found tended to freeze multiple times while scanning a short story, sometimes twice on the same page, requiring a restart of the computer, causing me to lose the pages already scanned. It took me an hour to read one submission out of six hundred, but I didn't say a word.

Jenny, my good friend from graduate school who was also a colleague, thought my recent course reduction might have resulted from my scarcity around the office. She made conversation with everyone, knew everybody's name. I never called anyone by their name, lest I guess incorrectly whom a voice belonged to. Last year Jenny was promoted to full-time lecturer.

I phoned disability services at the university, asked if they could provide screen-reading software. They seemed willing to help until I clarified that I was faculty, not a student. Why faculty blindness was considered different from student blindness made no sense. Then I remembered which of us wrote checks to the university.

Disability services referred me to human resources. HR directed me to my department chair. With budget cuts brought up in every faculty meeting, how many classes would I be assigned if I asserted my ADA right to software costing more than a thousand dollars?

Some critics complain that Tom Cruise only plays variations of Tom Cruise, but maybe no role can contain his outsized charisma. The archetypal Cruise hero takes shape in 1983's *Risky Business*. By the end of the film, Cruise's high school senior has found romance, riches, and admission to the Ivy League by turning his house into a brothel while his parents are out of town. Note the iconic Ray-Bans Cruise dons in the film's final minutes.

Sunglasses become a Cruise staple, returning in *Top Gun*, *Rain Man*, *Days of Thunder*, et al. As cool as the shades make him look, they are also a symbol of his imperviousness, shields against whatever life might throw his way. Sunglasses say, Maybe you see me, but you can't see what I see.

In *Rain Man*, after learning the heir to his father's estate is an autistic brother he didn't know he had, Cruise kidnaps him in hopes of claiming the inheritance. The trip west becomes a road trip when the autistic brother refuses to fly any airline other than Qantas, an Australian outfit that, as of the late 1980s, is the only airline that has never crashed. Interstates, too, are out of the question—too many annual fatalities. Even the matter of Hoffman's underwear requires special accommodations. On the highway, Hoffman reveals he is going commando, eschewing the briefs Cruise gave him because they did not come from the Kmart a few miles from his institution.

I explained all of this to a girl my senior year of college when we found my favorite movie on TV, already in progress. I was surprised she had never seen *Rain Man* before.

Cruise and Hoffman were in Las Vegas, descending the escalator in matching suits, when the new girl kissed me. Moments later, I pulled away.

"I can't drive," I told her.

She opened her eyes.

"I mean, I can't drive you around. I just think you should know."

"I'll drive you around," she said, and pulled me toward her.

She broke up with me amicably after a month and a half, the girl who didn't care that I couldn't drive. It seemed to have nothing to do with my vision, but anything can be ignored for a month, even a year. Six years, in fact, passed between my first and last kisses with the poet who was divorcing me.

"I don't want to hurt you," said Meredith the first time we kissed, and maybe that made hurting me inevitable. At the time, she was alluding to the British fellow to whom she was practically engaged. She didn't plan to break up with him, she reiterated, our clothes piling up on the floor.

"Don't worry about me," I said, trying to channel actors cooler than I had ever been: Luke Perry, Patrick Swayze, Brad Pitt. How could she hurt me? I was Tom fucking Cruise.

———

Meredith emailed to say the divorce papers would be arriving via certified mail. A large *X* would indicate the places I needed to sign. I had a method, when no one was around, of using my magnifier and check-writing guide to sign on a given line. Unfortunately, I had to sign these papers in the presence of a notary public.

The day after the papers came, I carried them up four flights of stairs in the university's administration building. There was a notary in payroll available to employees. In the past, I had always put off these kinds of tasks. Perhaps a quick turnaround would show Meredith I was a changed man.

A dark smudge behind the front desk might have been a receptionist's hair. I waited for a greeting. Sometimes one never came, but I preferred this to being caught speaking to an empty desk. That I might react to this with an easy smile and an explanation that I was visually impaired, that the weight of this confession was only as heavy as I made it seem, never occurred to me.

The notary led me to a small table. She was a tall, middle-aged woman. Her height I could see. Her age I thought I could hear, but lately I was less certain about these conclusions. Lately I was less certain that they ever mattered.

"My eyes are bad," I told her up front, knowing I'd need help signing on the lines. She held her finger on the edge of the page, asked if I could see the *X*. My system of magnifier and check-writing guide wasn't a show I performed for audiences.

My nose an inch from the page, I apologized for the delay. "The line comes into focus eventually," I said, the same lie I had been telling since I was seventeen. What was I trying to hide from this woman I would likely never see again? Why was I hiding it from anyone?

"It's okay," said the notary. She might have meant the time it was taking me to sign my name on four lines. She might have noticed some emotion in my eyes. I hadn't told her what these documents were that she was notarizing, but it couldn't have been hard to tell.

"When I was a kid and I got scared, the Rain Man would come and sing to me." Tom Cruise says this to his girlfriend early in the movie, almost to himself, believing the Rain Man had been an imaginary friend.

Halfway to California, when Hoffman refers to himself as Rain Man, Cruise realizes he had been trying to say his brother's name, Raymond, and it came out Rain Man. Hoffman remembers the song he used to sing, and the two duet softly to "I Saw Her Standing There." Cruise's prickly exterior finally gives way to empathy. He will take care of his brother, money or no money.

In the end, life outside the institution is too much for Raymond, and he returns to Cincinnati, but never mind that. Tom's girlfriend, who left him earlier in the movie, has taken him back. He has learned to love. His brother will always live in a world of his own, but after two hours and thirteen minutes, Tom Cruise is a new man.

And so I popped another Tom Cruise movie into the VCR, blind spots larger than the TV, borne back ceaselessly into the cinema of my youth. Nostalgia, I read somewhere, means the pain of a wound that hasn't healed, but that didn't sound right.

———

One spring afternoon, Matt talked me into attending a poetry reading. The poet was an alum of our writing program, a friend of his, but I hadn't known her well. Nor did I get excited about poetry readings, despite—or maybe a result of—having been married to a poet.

For half an hour, I sat in awe of her poems, most of them about the disability someone with better eyesight would have noticed while she was reading. To me, seated in the third row, she was only the lines of her poetry, each stanza a flag planted in the center of her life: This is me, and this is me, and this and this and this.

It was the first poetry collection I had bought since graduate school that wasn't a gift to my wife. The next day I scanned the pages into my computer, translating the text into digital speech. I read it in a sitting. I reread it later in the week, envious of how starkly, how boldly, each poem announced her difference.

"Why don't you write about losing your eyesight?" Jenny had asked me in graduate school after the weekly workshop.

I must have winced at her suggestion.

"You don't think it's interesting?"

I shook my head and changed the subject. A burnout of my optic nerves was a worse plot than the aimless novel I would abandon before graduation. More than this, the thought of readers, people I had never even met, knowing I was *blind*, *disabled*, felt like the opposite of why I chose to be a writer.

In 2008, a video surfaced of Tom Cruise extolling the virtues of Scientology. In a black turtleneck, between fits of impertinent laughter, he spoke in the acronyms and aphorisms of his New Age religion, a version of the *Mission: Impossible* theme playing in the background.

Tom Cruise fandom had gotten complicated in recent years. His couch gymnastics on *Oprah* when discussing new girlfriend Katie Holmes were one thing—if I were dating Katie Holmes, I'd jump on a couch, too—but his comments on the *Today* show were harder to overlook. He called Matt Lauer glib, a solid point, but then he labeled psychiatry a sham and condemned the use of antidepressants.

In the new viral video, with his patented smile, Tom said you were either on the playing field or out of the arena. "Now is the time," he said. "The time is now."

The Scientology thing had always given me pause. It seemed at best a self-help pyramid scheme, at worst a nefarious cult. Either way, it was hard to argue with the results. He was Tom Cruise. Who the hell was I?

The next fall, the department assigned me five sections of composition, one more than I had ever taught. The incoming freshman class was one of the biggest on record. Course size was raised from twenty-five to twenty-seven. The wary sigh I might have once exhaled at the prospect of grading 135 papers four times in fifteen weeks was one of relief.

My throat was raw after using my teaching voice for nearly five hours. I had never been happier to explicate a syllabus to blurry rows of desks. When blind spots and an inability to see hands going up was the only reason I gave for my policy of not raising hands, no one reacted. By my third class of the day, neither did I.

Sometimes, later in the semester, students asked about my eyes. They weren't hard questions. Over time, the answers came more easily.

The following spring, a letter from Social Security informed me I was no longer eligible for disability. I earned more than the monthly limit in order to receive checks. The news was not unexpected. I reread the paragraphs several times, though they made perfect sense.

Aside from a few outbursts, Dustin Hoffman's performance in *Rain Man* demands little range. Cruise portrays a character who changes, but Oscar has always had a soft spot for disability. Tom's first nomination came for playing paralyzed Vietnam veteran Ron Kovic in *Born on the Fourth of July*. He lost to Daniel Day-Lewis, who played a man with cerebral palsy in *My Left Foot*.

Many years after losing my sight, alone in that apartment with the crooked floors, I discovered the scene in *Rain Man* I wished I had shown during my high school presentation. Halfway into the film, right before the famous underwear scene, there's a moment when Dustin Hoffman breaks character. It had been a long time since I had seen the movie—seen it with my eyes—but I remembered it as clearly as my teenage face.

On the highway, Hoffman reiterates that he's an excellent driver. Cruise says he'll have to let him drive sometime, not meaning it, and Hoffman reaches for the wheel. The car swerves. Cruise screams at his brother, and a narrow grin flickers across Hoffman's face.

I used to think this was a mistake by the director, a wrong

take that should have been edited out. Now I wasn't so sure.
What if, I could have told my high school classmates—what
if, I wish I had told myself—Dustin Hoffman is smiling on
purpose? This strange man, he wants us to see, wants us to
believe, is capable of joy.

10

DATING TIPS FOR THOSE STILL IN DENIAL ABOUT THEIR DISABILITY

1. SHARE YOUR BIGGEST SECRET WITH A CRACKER BARREL CASHIER

Your stomach hasn't felt right since your wife asked for a divorce two weeks ago, but you should probably eat something. Matt reads you the restaurant names on road signs. He's driving the moving truck of your belongings back to North Carolina.

"I never thought I'd be thirty and divorced," you tell Matt over something called chicken-fried chicken at a Knoxville Cracker Barrel.

"Better than being thirty and unhappily married," says

Matt, who got engaged the same week you did. He's been single for two months.

You pick up the check and give your credit card to the cashier. She swipes your card, but you're not out of the woods yet. Instead of a receipt on which to scribble your illegible signature near the bottom, she directs your attention to a screen in front of the register.

For years, you memorized the buttons on these devices, but the differences between machines gradually made this impossible. Now touch screens present a whole new level of impossibility for the blind.

Matt pushes the pair of buttons to complete the transaction.

"My eyesight is bad," you tell the cashier, the first explanation you've ever offered for these moments you step aside.

On the way to the truck, Matt lays a hand on your back. "I've never heard you say that before."

More than your confession to the cashier, it's your friend's hand that prompts your first tears since leaving Nashville. Two weeks ago, you called him and two other friends, Ron and Jenny, explaining everything you had never explained to them—to anyone—hoping for advice that might save your marriage. In your mind, your closest friends have always accepted you in ways girlfriends never could. Maybe your friends never asked for more than you were willing to give.

2. LET GO

Since returning to North Carolina, you've only spoken to her by email, providing your new address, declining her offer to renew your shared Costco membership, asking if she's seen your *Nebraska* CD or that long-handled coffee scoop you got from Crate & Barrel in Raleigh after the Prince concert. You're proud of how nice you've been. The first day you returned to Greensboro, you bought her a Netflix subscription, the account you shared having been in your name. You thought you were trying to prove something to her, that you would like to remain friends, despite the fact that—or maybe because—you hadn't really been friends while you were a couple. But you've come to realize, even before you send her that out-of-print poetry collection for Christmas, that these gestures are more for your benefit than hers. What you hope is that each kindness makes her feel as small as you felt when she told you, in as many words, that a blind man could not make her happy.

Her email in late January lets you know it is done. Court documents will be arriving soon. Once you mailed back the papers, signed and notarized, your presence in the courtroom was not necessary.

Later in the week, the final decree arrives in a thick envelope. The legal language is comforting in its detachment. Even your name is a series of words, no more who you are than the sounds they make.

3. FALL IN LOVE WITH YOUR FRIEND'S SISTER

Over beers, one of your good friends says his sister thinks you're funny and cute. You've met her twice, and the feeling is mutual. She lives hours away in Virginia, but your friend's comment snowballs rapidly into a double date with his sister and one of her friends.

You have never felt less pressure on a first date. Knowing there's interest settles your nerves. Your familiarity through her brother leads to easy conversation over wine and steak. Snow has fallen in the hours you've been inside the restaurant, and you offer her your hand on the icy sidewalk. She's still holding it when the four of you file into the taxi.

You wake up in her bed, a hangover as bad as you've had since college. The pounding headache doesn't diminish the joy of waking up beside an attractive woman who gets all your jokes. After brunch, the two of you say your goodbyes, trading phone numbers and email addresses. Casually, or what you hope comes across as casually, you mention the possibility of taking a train to Richmond some weekend.

You manage to wait an entire day before calling her, leaving a long, rambling voice mail you hope she will find appealing in a Hugh Grant/Ben Stiller/John Cusack kind of way.

Two days go by before she returns your call, but it goes well. You think it went well. Did it go well? In an email a few days after the hour-long conversation, she expresses misgivings about the distance, her previous relationship having ended for that reason. But you're pretty sure it was your calling too soon. Unless, of course, it was something else.

4. TRY A LITTLE HARDER TO BE ALONE

You don't have to be in a relationship. People throughout history have lived fruitful, wondrous lives without the romantic love of another person. This is what you tell yourself as you authorize eHarmony to debit your bank account thirty dollars a month for the next six months. It's something to do, a way to extend your social circle. This is what you tell yourself as you complete your profile on the dating site whose TV ads taunt you with happy banter between married couples who met on the site.

The only pictures you have of yourself are on a DVD of wedding photos, probably not the most appropriate for a dating profile. Jenny provides some group pictures from recent years and has you smile for a head shot. You're curious if you managed to look directly at the camera but don't want to ask, don't want it to matter. Privately, your ex-wife instructed the wedding photographer to make sure you weren't looking off to the side.

A dating profile is, if not exactly a lie, a carefully constructed press release. How should you say you've been legally blind since you were sixteen? You could try to hide it, as you've done for so many years, but passing for sighted, you're finally able to admit, hasn't worked out as you hoped it would. In trying so hard not to be different, you've been a poor attempt at ordinary.

You type a few sentences about your disability in the *Other Things about Me* section. Hours later, you shorten what you wrote to a single sentence. Finally you delete it altogether and click SAVE.

5. TYPING IS NOT DATING

Within hours of completing your profile, multiple women initiate communication. This is encouraging for many reasons. Someone bold enough to make the first move might be okay with a man who can't drive. The first round of communication consists of five icebreaker questions so innocuous as to be virtually useless. One, for example, asks "How often do you like to laugh?" The multiple-choice answers range from "I like a good joke from time to time" to "I crack myself up!"

You're a little surprised, perhaps disappointed in yourself, at how much physical appearance factors into your early decisions. For your entire adult life, you've dreamed of the mythical love at first sight, of superficially picking a young lady out of a crowd, a bar, a bookstore. You've always had to go in reverse, getting to know someone before getting close enough for a thorough look at her face. This sounds romantic on paper, but let's face it: This method hasn't served you well.

When you can't get a good look at someone, which is most people you're not kissing, your mind has filled in the blurs from the finite gallery of faces you encountered before you lost your sight. Now you can hold your magnifier against the computer screen and evaluate, inaccurately but with less guessing than in person, physical beauty. If someone's profile pics bear little resemblance to her actual appearance, your letdown won't be any different from sighted people deceived by flattering lighting.

Are you being shallow not to respond to the woman in what is either a purple kimono or a sorceress costume who looks like your eighth-grade journalism teacher? Perhaps. But how much compatibility can there be with a woman who has answered beneath *The Last Book I Read*, "I don't really read!!"? Her use of two exclamation points will unsettle you for some time.

The same shallow impulse pushes you to respond to a

nurse in her twenties named Soledad. Her primary profile pic seems to have been taken two hours after sunset, from at least twenty yards away, but you've always had a thing for the former CNN anchor Soledad O'Brien.

After trading lists of traits you're looking for in a partner comes the exchange of open-ended questions. You try not to judge typos or poorly worded answers—the last thing you're looking for is another writer—but you can tell a lot from the words someone uses. Soledad's use of "tee hee," for example, after sentences that don't strike you as attempts at humor, hint at a deep incompatibility. One can also tell a lot from what isn't said. One of your matches, for example, might infer something like denial from the omission of your blindness from your profile. She might also deduce from such an omission that it's not a big deal, or doesn't have to be. For someone who's supposed to be good with words, you still can't find the right ones to tell strangers who you are and who you are not.

6. KEEP AN OPEN MIND

Every woman with whom you interact seems to possess one flaw that, like a loose thread, causes your hypothetical future together to unravel. The tall, red-haired marketing executive with a photo of herself on roller skates loves to read novels whose covers have puffy letters, the kind they sell at airport newsstands. For ambiguous emphasis, she adds a punctuation smiley face. The veterinarian has three dogs, which seems like one too many for a single person. The accountant who loves eighties music—that sounds promising—has an odd way of spelling her otherwise common first name, and why is she sitting on the lap of the dapper fellow captioned *best friend* in that last photo? Too many exclamation points in a profile? Pass. (Note: Two exclamation points are too many exclamation points!) References to oneself as a "picky eater" foretell a lot of dinners at Applebee's and Olive Garden. Mentions of a love of dancing, when the age listed is over twenty-four, suggest a freer spirit than you might be able to wrangle in your thirties.

You don't rule out anyone who wants children, a question so important the site puts it beneath everyone's age. Your ex-wife did not want kids, but days before you left Nashville she told you maybe she did want kids, just not with you. A long silence followed. Both of you knew what she meant. Your profile lists you as a maybe on children. Maybe more than kids, you want someone to find you worthy of parenthood. Maybe you're more enamored of possibility and hypothetical futures than the terror of actually meeting these people. Maybe if you keep saying no, none of them can reject you.

7. YOU'VE DONE THIS BEFORE

Your first date is with a Russian graduate student in psychology named Svetlana. Her suggestion of getting coffee is a disappointment and a relief. Coffee, you're fairly certain, is not a real date.

You arrive twenty minutes early, ensuring she will have to look for you. The alternative is not an option. You mentioned your eyesight in one of your emails, nestling it in the sentence about not being able to drive. You're the one to bring it up again over evening coffee, and she asks a few questions, nods, shifts the conversation back to her divorce. To have something to say, you find yourself offering details of your own divorce. An hour and a half later, you shake hands outside the coffee shop.

"How did it go?" asks Jenny.

"Pretty well," you say, knowing you'll never see Svetlana again.

"Don't you love meeting new people?" asks the most outgoing friend you've ever had.

You do not, in fact, enjoy meeting new people. For two days prior to this date, you were so nervous you came close to vomiting several times. Your freshman year of college, this same anxiety led to the loss of twenty pounds. Meeting strangers might be less stressful if you weren't trying to convince them, with body language if not words, that you are not blind.

In the interest of keeping your inbox filled, you join OkCupid, a free dating site with a more casual atmosphere than the marriage-centric ethos of eHarmony. Within hours of setting up your account, a self-described writer with a striking resemblance to a young Stockard Channing sends you a two-word message: *Nice Profile*. You're not sure how to interpret this in light of the line in her profile that states, "I'm mostly looking for women. Mostly."

You write back, complimenting her taste in music. She lives in Durham, an hour away, but doesn't balk at your upfront admission that you can't drive. She generously offers to meet you for tapas in Greensboro. She has an MFA in fiction from a well-regarded school in Massachusetts, a love of pop culture, and a dry sense of humor. After parting outside the restaurant with a chaste hug, you're surprised to hear from her the next day via email. She mentions a food festival the following weekend. It's blocks from your apartment. You'd love to, of course, but you worry about the distance between your two cities.

While communicating with women in the neighboring towns of High Point and Winston-Salem, twenty and thirty miles away, respectively, you looked into trains that went there but have taken no initiative to try them out. Convenient as your apartment is to downtown Greensboro, you haven't even bothered with the city bus. Your ex-wife believed your aversion to the bus limited your independence. Your response, that paying someone to drive you around the city was less independent than walking somewhere on your own two feet, probably didn't prove her wrong.

After the food festival, you grab a drink at your regular bar. Young Stockard Channing doesn't ask follow-ups about your eyes. You kind of wish she would because bringing it up yourself, apropos of nothing, feels like it might contradict the *so what* message you're trying to send. For three hours, topics of conversation have included favorite books, childhood pets, *The A-Team* and *ALF*. The date, if that's what it was, concludes with a less thorough hug inside her car with your seat belts on. In the coming days, you wonder if you should offer to go to Durham, but you stop short of checking the train schedule. Maybe you should wait for her to invite you. Were these even dates? When emails peter out, you decide you had mostly been hanging out. Mostly.

8. THINK OF A TRAUMATIC EXPERIENCE

Inspired by the film *Sideways*, Ron suggests the two of you go on a guys' vacation through wine country. Like the characters in the film, you and he were the best man at each other's weddings, but Ron remains happily married. You, on the other hand, remind yourself a little too much of the divorced, unpublished novelist played by Paul Giamatti. Perhaps Los Angeles would be more festive.

A few weeks before your trip, Ron stumbles across a *New Yorker* article about the Church of Scientology's Celebrity Centre, a turreted castle on three acres once known as the Château Élysée. In Hollywood's golden age, regular guests of the architectural landmark included Errol Flynn, Carole Lombard, and Cary Grant. According to the website, the center offers free tours to the public as well as a delightful brunch. One of the characters in your novel, the one you haven't touched in nine months, is a member of a New Age religion inspired by Scientology. A visit would be terrific research.

Between trips to the brunch buffet, you and Ron observe Scientologists in their natural habitat. At a neighboring table, middle-aged women who seem plucked from a book club keep saying *org* and *tech*. Out the dining room windows, Ron notices women in white blouses and navy slacks filing out of an adjacent building. More than once, the waiter startles you with stealthy refills of your coffee. After brunch, you ask a receptionist about the free tour. She places a phone call, and a woman in a white blouse and navy slacks arrives to take you upstairs.

Your tour guide is a brunette in cat-eye glasses named Desiree. You've never met a white woman named Desiree. Is she white? You often don't notice ethnicity. Desiree asks for your name and mailing address, which you provide without hesitation. Ron gives her a fake name and the address of his first apartment in Pittsburgh. Leading the two of you down the hall of the former hotel, Desiree explains the basics of Scientology, that it is not a faith but a practice, not something one *believes* but one *does*.

"Is either of you a creative person?"

"Failed novelist," you joke, trying to chip away at Desiree's icy veneer.

Your tour guide does not laugh. She explains the high regard in which Scientology founder L. Ron Hubbard held all artists. The founder's office remains as he left it, says Desiree, gesturing to an open door—in case he ever returns, Ron read somewhere.

In a large, sunny room, she steps behind a small table and asks if you've ever heard of an E-meter. You've read about the free "stress test" you're about to receive, but you play dumb. Eagerly you wrap your hands around cylinders the size of soda cans.

"Think of a traumatic experience," Desiree says.

Closing your eyes, you recall a friend's recent critique of your novel.

Desiree seems unimpressed.

You try again, conjuring a road trip with your ex-wife. Unable to read the MapQuest directions quickly enough with your 22× magnifier, you were startled when she snatched the pages from your hand and, finding the exit number, tossed them in the backseat.

"Wow," says Desiree. "That was a big one."

"That was an ex-wife thought," you say, proud of the impression you've made on the fabled E-meter.

"Care to elaborate?"

You laugh, pretend it's a rhetorical question. You don't mind telling strangers you're divorced. It's the other traumatic experience you'd rather not describe.

To your mild disappointment, you are not whisked through a hidden doorway for hours of brainwashing. Tom Cruise, your boyhood idol, does not greet you with his booming, infectious laugh. Desiree leads you to their bookstore and tells you how to learn more about the church if you're interested. You're not ready to leave, but the tour is over. You remind yourself this was only research for your novel.

On the way to the car, Ron checks his phone. "I got it."

"Got what?"

"Your picture with the E-meter. I had to angle it so she wouldn't see. Your head's cut off, but you can tell it's you."

9. DON'T BE SO SHALLOW

More matches, more emails, more dates. The low point comes with the former flight attendant who shares your ex-wife's first name. Her profile contains few details—she has left most sections blank—but in her only photo she smiles sexily with her head to one side. Matt warned you about profiles with only one picture and scant information. One of his matches fitting this description, after initiating communication, asked immediately for his credit card number.

It's hard to tell if you have anything in common. At this point, you're tired of caring. When the girl with the sexy smile doesn't ask for your credit card, you make plans to meet.

You're at the Irish pub when she calls to say she'll be a few minutes late. A few means forty, but a low-cut top and tight jeans make for a great apology. On your way to the patio, a sloshed fellow on a barstool compliments you on her appearance.

"I'll be right back," says the former flight attendant.

You've been talking for fifteen minutes under the stars of late spring, the quiet din of downtown traffic over your shoulder. Five minutes go by. Ten. Fifteen. Her departure from the table came around the time you joked about how little adjunct instructors are paid. Before that, you unburdened yourself of the most basic details of your visual impairment. She asked no questions. All she has told you, really, is how much she loved her recent trip to wine country.

You're somewhat surprised when she returns. She says a friend has been texting. The friend is going through something, the former flight attendant begins to explain, and you cut her off with a smile and an extended hand.

"It was lovely meting you."

"You, too," she says.

You pay for her drink, a twenty-one-dollar ale she might have sipped twice. Perhaps love at first sight isn't the answer.

10. GIVE UP

With some of your matches, you have long phone conversations. You are interested in them. They are interested in you, or at least in the charming fellow you can be on the phone. There has to be some compatibility between people who talk on the phone for three hours, and yet you're not sure either of you is saying anything that matters. In the early days of getting to know your ex-wife, she said you were very good on the phone, and years later, that you used it as a crutch.

Why can't you crack the code that gets you past first and second dates to the stage where you meet each other's friends? It's tempting to blame the formality of dating, online or otherwise, its stilted procedures and lofty expectations. Friends' stories of their awful dates remind you this isn't easy for anyone.

Maybe all your false starts have little or nothing to do with your disability. Sometimes you wonder if another person is what you're looking for. When your six-month membership to the dating website expires, you don't renew.

11. TRY NOT TO SEARCH FOR METAPHORS AT THE GYM

Five or six days a week you hoist heavy bars away from your body, pull on handles attached to cables, pushing weight as far from your chest as it will go.

Running laps on the indoor track is your preferred cardio. Nine laps around the inside lane make up a mile. Prior to this year, you've never run farther than two miles. Your body wasn't made for running, you told your high school gym teacher. Exercise wouldn't be anything but good for you, he had said, skeptical of the doctor's note from your ophthalmologist that didn't actually say what you couldn't do. Soon you're running three miles, or twenty-seven laps. Then four miles. Five. A real accomplishment, you think, turning the corner of your forty-fifth consecutive circle.

12. ACCEPT A RIDE FROM A STRANGER

Why hipsters and some of your friends love dive bars you don't quite understand, but peer pressure compels you to join them for one beer before calling it a night. It's the tavern with a selection of two draft beers served in plastic cups and a bathroom without a flushing toilet. You've been here no more than ten minutes when Jenny summons you to the end of the bar. She and her boyfriend have already struck up a conversation with strangers.

"The girl in the purple top is single," Jenny whispers in your ear. "She seems really nice."

The single girl is also here with a couple, a former minor-league baseball player and a grad student in sociology. You chat sports with the former baseball player. When Bell Biv DeVoe's "Poison" comes on the jukebox, you and the baseball player's girlfriend parse the origins of the term *new jack swing*.

The single girl, when your four couple friends shift positions so the two of you are beside each other, is much less talkative. She brightens slightly when discussing her afternoon picking strawberries at a local farm, but you're not able to elevate this into conversation.

All your friends left half an hour ago, as did the friends of the single girl. Convinced this is going nowhere, you set your plastic cup on the bar. To your surprise, the single girl asks if you want a ride home. She assures you she only had one drink two hours ago.

"Oh, I'm fine. I just live a few blocks away."

"It's no problem."

"Really. I'm just literally three blocks down Mendenhall."

"I don't mind," she says with a laugh that makes your insistence on walking feel problematic.

You follow her to a pale sedan. After fastening your seat belt, your fingers furtively locate the door handle. The last thing you want is to embarrass yourself with a prolonged search for it when she drops you off. At the West Market Mendenhall traffic light, you prepare to tell her which driveway is yours. It would have been easier to walk, not to worry about door handles and seeing your own building well enough in the dark to tell an ostensible stranger where to let you out. She pulls into the driveway of the house beside yours. Close enough.

"It was nice meeting you," you say.

"Yeah. You, too."

Only now, in the silence before you get out of the car, does it occur to you that this single girl might have offered you a ride to continue your awkward conversation from the bar. No evidence supports this, but for some reason you say . . .

"If I had something to write with, I'd give you my phone number."

She makes an indeterminate sound.

One of your friends, when recounting his dates, determines a woman's interest based on her eye contact. Because you never had a girlfriend when you were able to see eyes—with apologies to Julie Schiffman, sixth grade doesn't count—you're not sure what he looks for. It's possible you're missing signals. Perhaps in trying to hold someone's gaze, you're failing to communicate your own interest. It's worth noting that this friend remains single.

If you were a more confident man, you would invite the single girl in for a drink, the way people do in movies. But you have never been that guy, have never operated with the confidence of the physically attractive, have never believed a woman could fall for you because of your looks. You utter an unconvincing *see you later* and wave from the sidewalk to the single girl.

13. REACTIVATE YOUR ONLINE DATING ACCOUNTS LIKE YOU JUST DON'T CARE

For your second attempt at online dating, you select the one-month-at-a-time plan. The thrills that once accompanied emails from eHarmony are long gone. You are a gambler out for revenge against the casino that took his life savings.

In short order, you reach open communication with two matches: a PhD student in English named Laurie and a graphic designer named Lori. Open communication. It's a feat not to roll your eyes at that deceptive label. Both Laurie and Lori seem attractive. Both like to read. Both have a cat, which feels important. Although you don't have a cat, you had two as a child. In your profile, trying to describe the ineffable sweetness or empathy you'd most like to find in a partner, you said you are looking for someone who would stop to pet a cat.

Of Laurie and Lori, the latter is the first to send you a message in open communication. "What now?" reads the entirety of her email.

14. ATTEND THE WEDDING OF YOUR OLDEST FRIEND

Rizwan is one of the last friends you tell about your divorce. Daily phone calls in your teens and early twenties have dwindled to catching up on each other's birthdays. Telling him you're getting divorced isn't as hard as explaining why.

"That makes sense," he says.

In your oldest friend's lack of surprise, you hear how obvious your charade has always been, even if you've never talked about it. Riz lost his father the same year you lost your sight, and you never talked about that either. There was nothing to say, you thought, but maybe you didn't have the words.

Riz is glad you called. The girl you met a few years ago, his classmate from medical school, recently became his fiancée. Would you be one of his groomsmen at the wedding?

There's an Islamic ceremony for Riz's family on Friday, followed by a Christian ceremony Saturday evening. When you arrive for the former, Riz's baby brother and kid sister greet you with big hugs. His aunt and uncle and cousin all remember you from trips to the beach. This feeling, you realize, as if there's never been a time people didn't know you, is what's been missing from all your dates.

You've met Riz's fiancée only once, but she feels like a part of your shared history. Riz has filled her in on all the stories and inside jokes of your twenty-year friendship. He used to be so shy, so reticent to talk about himself.

The first ceremony feels like the rehearsal. Traditional garments made by Riz's relatives in Pakistan fit some members of the wedding party better than others. No one is sure where to stand. Riz's uncle officiates, asking the bride and groom to repeat after him. Line after line, they botch pronunciations, breaking into occasional chuckles.

Most guests attend the second ceremony. You watch from the side of the stage while Riz's brother, now in college, hands him the ring. Today the bride and groom exchange vows they have written themselves, sobbing while they speak. You wipe away tears, the first time you've cried at a wedding, including your own. It isn't their sobs or the words they read from index cards, but the times they pause to collect themselves, in the brief silence, when you hear how much they have shared.

15. SING, EVEN THOUGH YOU'VE JUST MET

A pair of phone conversations with Lori go well—they always do—and you make plans for dinner. Upon learning she lives blocks away, in an apartment fifty feet from that dive bar to which you'll never return, you suggest a restaurant the two of you can walk to. Long-term romance between a graphic designer and a blind writer feels like a long shot, but how about the exceptionally average Thai Garden on Tate Street?

You love pad Thai but are disinclined to order it because it is such a common dish, the spaghetti and meatballs of Thai cuisine. To hell with it. You order pad Thai, and so does Lori.

She seems tentative—you both do—but not nervous. You prefer this to the carefully built wall of enthusiasm you've encountered on so many first dates. Conversation comes easily. Every detail of her life story creates more conversational hypertext you want to click on. For two years she worked for a traveling carnival in Southern California. She left home at age sixteen, played guitar in a punk band, hitchhiked and hopped trains in the Pacific Northwest. Her father was a Scientologist. The stories emerge slowly and out of order because, for some reason, she is interested in the humdrum narrative of your own life. She asks about the novel you're working on. You don't like to talk about works in progress, but you find yourself summarizing the plot and main characters.

"That sounds fascinating," she says. "Have you ever read *Geek Love?*"

Your eyes widen. Katherine Dunn's novel about Depression-era carnies is one of Lori's favorites. Yours, too. It's also the biggest inspiration for the book you've been working on for over two years.

Dinner leads to coffee across the street, where you used to stop before morning classes. Familiar as you are with this strip of storefronts bordering the university, your date knows it even better. In her early teens, she was one of the misfit kids found on the sidewalks of Tate Street at all hours, nicknamed Tater Tots. Their presence was as constant as the homeless with whom the teens often hung out. This she won't tell you tonight, but next week on your second date. That night, while walking downtown for dessert, she will seem embarrassed when a man smoking in front of an old apartment building engages her in conversation. She explains how she knew him, alluding to the "punk rock lifestyle" she cited when you asked in an email why she doesn't drink. The gray tones of regret color some of her stories, but she never has trouble finding the words.

"When you say punk rock, do you mean like pink hair and Mohawks?" you ask.

"Something like that."

"Any body piercings?"

"Not anymore."

"Ever shave your head?"

"Kind of."

"Wow. I can't imagine you calling that much attention to yourself."

"It's not about attention, really. More like hiding parts of yourself behind a costume."

Your first date approaches the top of its fourth hour, and you have yet to leave Tate Street Coffee House. Topics of conversation shuffle wildly, leading you somehow to the 1980s song "One Night in Bangkok." Lori doesn't know the song and, to your surprise, you hear yourself singing the chorus.

"Doesn't ring a bell?"

She laughs, still certain she's never heard it.

You sing a little more. Are you actually snapping your fingers?

The two of you end up at your apartment, talking and talking over glasses of water. Not drinking on a date is a new one for you. Somehow you're more at ease without the artificial comfort of a wine buzz. Even your coffee was decaf, unaware when you ordered that you'd be up for a long, long time.

You brought up your blindness during open communication. The subject doesn't arise on your date until dawn brightens the windows of your bedroom. Lori asks, in as many words, what you can see and what you can't. Sooner or later, this question always comes.

"It's hard to explain," you say, surprising yourself. This isn't your standard response.

What follows is more detailed than your typical debriefing, and for some time you'll wonder how it came out differently this time, as effortlessly as a song.

16. DON'T SAY YOU'RE SORRY

A few dates in, the mood over breakfast seems to shift. Lori has to tell you something. If it were something you wanted to hear, it probably wouldn't require a preface. Already both of you have deactivated your dating profiles. Early as it is, you're surprised, during her long pause to steel herself, to discover there is already something to lose.

She tells you what she needed to tell you. Is this all? you wonder. It isn't nothing, but it was harder for her to say than it was for you to hear. This seems to be the case whenever you confess what you can't see.

Leaving the bagel shop, Lori asks if you'd mind running into Target with her to pick up a few things. No problem. You need shampoo and some other items yourself, you blurt out before realizing what you've done. Oh well. It took you many months to learn the extent of your ex's impatience in these scenarios. If shopping together is going to be a problem, better to find out now.

You tell her which shampoo you use, the brand's blue-capped bottles seeming to multiply while you look. A few seconds go by. Five, six, seven, eight. You're holding your breath, feeling this new relationship begin to fray. At last she finds your shampoo and places it in the cart.

"Sorry," you say.

"Sorry for what?"

Your toothpaste is harder to locate. Why do they constantly move everything? "It doesn't matter," you say. "Any Colgate is fine."

"There it is." She places your toothpaste in the cart.

"Sorry," you say again.

"You don't have to apologize," she says.

17. ASK QUESTIONS

In the fall, Lori begins the bachelor's program in graphic design at the school where you earned your MFA. The campus is blocks from both your apartments. One evening after dinner, you show her around, pointing out buildings where her classes will be.

At twenty-nine, she was the oldest in her orientation. In the throes of the semester, she'll wish for the luxury of being a full-time student. At the same time, she'll find she appreciates her classes more than her fellow freshmen, certainly more than you did when you were eighteen.

"This will all make more sense when you're older," you sometimes joke with your first-year students, not really joking.

After you show her the art building, Lori asks if you can swing by the school's art museum next door. There's a Japanese woodblock exhibit she's been wanting to see.

You aren't the ideal patron of most museums, but you've always loved the reverent silence. Lori points to a piece she adores. You stare at the shadows and shapes for a period consistent with appreciating art. Are you pretending you can see it? Don't do that.

"What do you like about it?" it occurs to you to ask.

It takes her a moment to figure out how to describe it. In a few hours, you won't remember what she said, only how patiently she searched for the words. In five years, you'll peer into the Grand Canyon the day after your wedding, and the awe in Lori's voice will make words unnecessary.

18. REVISE

True revision, you tell your writing students, is more than correction. You might find yourself deleting entire pages, rewriting from a different point of view, changing past tense to present, overhauling your entire first draft upon discovering you hadn't known what you were trying to say until the last few paragraphs. Let's break down the word, you say, drawing a slash between *Re* and *Vision*. You're trying to see what you've written a second time, see it with fresh eyes, as you haven't seen it before.

At last you return to your novel. Three years have gone

by since you began writing it. Most of it needs to be rewritten, far more than readers of the first draft recommended. Draft by draft, the novel changes shape, becomes less and less recognizable from what it used to be. Few lines remain from the first pages you printed. Even the plot, which you had thought was working well enough, needs to be overhauled, but you're getting close. You can glimpse the story you're trying to tell.

11

BASKETBALL

AT THE UNIVERSITY REC CENTER, where I work out on an alumni membership, the indoor track circles three full-length basketball courts. During the school year, the ceiling echoes with the squeak of high-tops and the clang of errant three-pointers. Throughout the summer, the courts are relatively empty, allowing my podcasts and audiobooks to play at a lower volume. These days I can listen to both on a device the size of a deck of cards.

I always loved tennis and basketball, not that I was good at either. In two seasons of preteen hoops, I made two layups. The highlight of my tennis career was a mixed-doubles victory in a YMCA summer league. Our opponents, in their first month of the sport, held their rackets like flyswatters. But there was something deeply satisfying in the dimpled leather against the fingers before a jump shot, in the pop of a tennis ball against racket strings.

One summer afternoon, the rec center courts are empty. After two quiet laps around the track, I find myself approaching the counter for checking out equipment.

It's the first time I've held a basketball—I do the math—in twenty-one years. The feel of it, rough and smooth, familiar and new, makes me giddy as I descend the stairs. White vinyl curtains separate the three courts. I take my ball to the one at the far end.

I dribble slowly from one basket to the other. A few minutes go by before I think to shoot. I try a jumper from the top of the key. This will become, other than free throws, the shot I'm able to hit most often. *Most often* means two or three out of fifty attempts. My first shot after two decades away from the game bounces hard off the glass.

I chase down the rebound and hoist up a prayer, as they say, from behind half-court. Judging from the ball's echo against the wall, I believe I've missed by several feet.

Imagining defenders in pursuit, I sprint toward the basket, an athlete who's overcome a career-ending injury. How many times have I circled these courts while running? Asking for a basketball never occurred to me.

One day a kid is yelling from the court behind me. "Do you want to play?"

I call out to him, "My eyes are bad."

The kid is walking toward me, dribbling. "Do what?"

I have to shout above the noise of a pickup game on the next court. "I'm visually impaired. All I'm good for is shooting."

"Oh. No worries."

The walk home from the rec center requires me to cross seven streets. All have lights or stop signs. Times I arrive at an intersection where traffic is already stopped, I wait for the next light cycle. On residential streets, when lawn mowers or leaf blowers prevent me from hearing cars, I find somewhere quieter to cross.

"Why did Socrates believe wisdom is knowing what we don't know?" asked my freshman philosophy professor on our first exam. I don't remember what I wrote. Close as our desks were in that room, I took few notes. Most days I let myself be counted absent, fearful of signing my name over another student's on the attendance sheet.

Without the benefit of eye contact, I'm never sure when drivers are waiting for me to cross. I wave them on so there's no confusion. I have never had a death wish, though a history of horns and close calls suggests otherwise. Wisdom, it turns out, is acknowledging where I cannot go without help. Asking for help means I will never be independent, but how many of us truly are?

"You're soaking wet," Lori says when I get home.

It's summer in North Carolina, but I'm more drenched than I usually am when I return from the gym. Smiling a little—looking pretty pleased with myself, I'm sure—I tell my wife what I've been up to.

She's excited by this development. "I want to play basketball with you," she says.

Days later, we make our way to the rec center's farthest court. Five feet and zero inches, Lori played soccer and softball as a kid, but she has become a big fan of my West Virginia Mountaineers.

I show her where to place her hands. She finds better luck with her own unorthodox grip. We take turns shooting. She asks if I'm ready before sending a bounce pass in my direction. Bounce passes are the only kind I can handle.

One after another, we launch wild jumpers and crooked free throws. Our layups don't touch the rim. We spend a lot of time retrieving our ball from the adjacent court, laughing at all our misses. Every once in a while a three-pointer rattles in, and we scream our heads off, champions after a last-second shot.

ACKNOWLEDGMENTS

THIS BOOK COULD NOT have landed in better hands than those of my editor, Amy Cherry. I cannot thank you enough, Amy, for seeing the value in my story and for improving it in so many ways.

A long and winding path led me to my agent, Eric Smith, whose wisdom and empathy guided this book into its final shape. Thank you for believing in this book and in me. You are the best.

I began writing this memoir shortly after *Literary Hub* published the first essay I ever wrote about losing my sight. Thank you, Jonny Diamond, for helping me hear my own voice. Your continued support has meant the world.

This book benefited immeasurably from the insights of generous readers I am lucky to call friends. M. C. Armstrong, Beth Bates, Laura Carney, Paul Crenshaw, Karen Meadows, and Dina L. Relles offered invaluable feedback on parts or all of the manuscript. Your enthusiasm, too, was invaluable while completing a book that was not easy to complete.

The editors of literary magazines who published work from this book provided encouragement when it was greatly needed. For your insights and belief, thank you to Lauren Alwan and Lindsey Griffin of *The Museum of Americana*, Erin Stalcup of *Waxwing*, Barrie Jean Borich of *Slag Glass City*, Ilana Masad and Ashley Strosnider of *Prairie Schooner*, and Aaron Burch of *Hobart*.

Everyone at W. W. Norton has been a dream. Thank you to Zarina Patwa, Bee Holekamp, Sarahmay Wilkinson, Gabby Nugent, Meredith McGinnis, Amy Robbins, and so many others for treating my book with such care.

Thank you to my parents, Jim and Belinda, whose belief in my abilities has never wavered. Another definition of faith is not trying to change your son's mind when he says he wants to be a writer.

Lastly and always, thank you to Lori, my first reader, who makes every story easier to tell.